"Practical advice from a leader who has 'been there!' What is better than learning from experience? Learning from someone else's experience—get Scrappy!"
Marshall Goldsmith, Author of *The New York Times* bestsellers *MOJO* and *What Got You Here Won't Get You There*

"More than thirty thousand business books are published each year, but reading them should not be boring! Why read a boring management book when you can read Scrappy General Management?!"
Hannah Kain, CEO, ALOM Technologies, Inc.

"Most organizations assume—wrongly—that by the time people get to the position of General Manager, they know exactly what to do at every turn. In fact, more young professionals are entering executive ranks every year, and they need practical, concrete advice and guidance on specific situations they're facing today. Scrappy General Management doesn't beat around the bush and doesn't bore you with management theory. It provides fast solutions for a fast-paced world."
Alexandra Levit, Author of *MILLENNIALtweet: 140 Bite-Sized Ideas for Managing the Millennials*

Scrappy General Management

Common Sense Practices to Avoid Calamities, Catastrophes, and Lackluster Results

For Corporations and Small Businesses

By Michael Horton

A Happy About® series
20660 Stevens Creek Blvd., Suite 210,
Cupertino, CA 95014

Copyright © 2010 by Michael Horton

All rights reserved. No part of this book shall be reproduced, stored in a retrieval system, or transmitted by any means electronic, mechanical, photocopying, recording, or otherwise without written permission from the publisher.

Published by Scrappy About™, a Happy About® series
20660 Stevens Creek Blvd., Suite 210, Cupertino, CA 95014
http://scrappyabout.com

First Printing: October 2010
Paperback ISBN: 978-1-60005-148-7 (1-60005-148-0)
eBook ISBN: 978-1-60005-149-4 (1-60005-149-9)
Place of Publication: Silicon Valley, California, USA
Paperback Library of Congress Number: 2010930804

Trademarks

All terms mentioned in this book that are known to be trademarks or service marks have been appropriately capitalized. Scrappy About™ cannot attest to the accuracy of this information. Use of a term in this book should not be regarded as affecting the validity of any trademark or service mark. Scrappy About™ is a trademark of Happy About®. Scrappy Guides™ and Scrappy General Management™ are trademarks of Wiefling Consulting, LLC. Scrappy About™ is a Happy About® series.

Warning and Disclaimer

Every effort has been made to make this book as complete and as accurate as possible, but no warranty of fitness is implied. The information provided is on an "as is" basis. The author(s) and the publisher shall have neither liability nor responsibility to any person or entity with respect to any loss or damages arising from the information contained in this book.

Author's Note

How in the heck did I get to be a General Manager? Through a most unlikely combination of luck, fearlessness, and chutzpah! The incumbent GM resigned and I thought, "Well... it's now or never." I had a mixed bag of experience and a "bee in my bonnet." I called the CEO, who was in Sydney, Australia, a 5-hour flight away from our outback offices in Perth, and announced with confidence that I was going to stand in as the GM. I added in no uncertain terms that if he didn't like it, he'd need to get on a plane in order to kick me out of the office. He laughed and agreed. Knowing that this was a $100m/year business, I immediately started sweating bullets. But from that point on, I was selling—both myself and our company's services—and practicing my ABCs (Always Be Closing... the deal that is). Luckily, success ensued, and a few months later I was awarded the job permanently.

So why this book? When I started in the GM role, I had little idea of what a GM was meant to do. The title does give you a good hint as to what's required; kind of like General Electric tells you the company has something to do with electricity. But one thing's for sure, I couldn't ask my boss, as I'd just spent a good deal of time convincing him that I knew what I was doing so that I could get the job. While there is a plethora of literature on the different aspects of leadership, management, and marketing, it is rarely brought together in a useful form. A wise person once said, "There is no such thing as coincidence." If something works once, and you understand the how's and why's, there's a damn good chance you can get it to work again. And if the concept also happens by some stroke of luck to agree with some sort of academic theory, then by classic triangulation you have something that perhaps is worth documenting.

It doesn't matter if you're working in good times or bad, at the end of the day solid, common-sense management practice will serve you and your team well and allow you to achieve the results that you deserve. So enjoy the book, and I hope it helps you avoid calamities and produce results that are far from "lackluster."

Stay Scrappy!
– Michael

Meet the Scrappy Guides™

The Scrappy Guides™ is a series of books to help you accomplish the impossible. Those of you who say it can't be done should stay out of the way of those of us doing it!

Scrappy means ATTITUDE.

Scrappy means not relying on a title to be a leader.

Scrappy means being willing to take risks and put yourself out there.

Scrappy means doing the right thing, even when you don't feel like it.

Scrappy means having the steely resolve of a street fighter.

Scrappy means sticking to your guns even if you're shaking in your boots.

Scrappy means being committed beyond reason to making a difference.

Scrappy means caring about something more than you care about being comfortable, socially acceptable, or politically correct.

Scrappy means being absolutely, totally committed to extraordinary results.

Scrappy means EDGY! and is your edge in achieving outrageous results even when they seem impossible.

The Scrappy Guides™ help you muster the courage and commitment to pursue your goals—even when there is no evidence that you can succeed. They are your shield against the naysayers who will try to undermine you, and they will give you comfort during the inevitable failures that accompany most worthy pursuits. When you fail, fail fast, fail forward, in the direction of your goals, lurching fitfully if you must. Sometimes success is built on the foundation of a very tall junk pile.

Let's get scrappy!

The Books in the Scrappy Guides™ Series

Kimberly Wiefling
Scrappy Project Management: *The 12 Predictable and Avoidable Pitfalls Every Project Faces*

Julie Abrams, Carole Amos, Eldette Davie, Mai-Huong Le, Hannah Kain, Sue Lebeck, Terrie Mui, Pat Obuchowski, Yuko Shibata, Nathalie Udo, Betty Jo Waxman, Kimberly Wiefling
Scrappy Women in Business: *Living Proof That Bending the Rules Isn't Breaking the Law*

Michael Seese
Scrappy Information Security: *The Easy Way to Keep the Cyber Wolves at Bay*
Scrappy Business Contingency Planning: *How to Bullet-Proof Your Business and Laugh at Volcanoes, Tornadoes, Locust Plagues, and Hard Drive Crashes*

Michael Horton
Scrappy General Management: *Common Sense Practices to Avoid Calamities, Catastrophes, and Lack Luster Results for Corporations and Small Businesses*

Meet the Scrappy Guides™ Executive Editor

Kimberly Wiefling, Executive Editor of the Scrappy About Series, is a proven expert in enabling people to achieve what seems impossible but is merely difficult. She is the author of one of the top project-management books in the U.S., *Scrappy Project Management: The 12 Predictable and Avoidable Pitfalls Every Project Faces*, a book growing in popularity around the world and recently published in Japanese by Nikkei Business Press. She founded Wiefling Consulting, LLC, a global leadership and business management consulting firm, in 2001. She currently spends about half of her time working with high-potential leaders in Japanese companies as the Executive Director for ALC Education's Global Management Consulting Group, an organization based in Tokyo, Japan. Her work includes facilitating leadership, communication, teamwork, innovation, and execution excellence workshops to enable Japanese companies to solve global problems profitably.

A physicist by education, she began her professional career with ten years at HP in product development, project management, and engineering leadership. She spent five years in the wild and wacky world of Silicon Valley startups, including a Xerox Parc spinoff where she was the VP of Program Management. In 2001, she rose from the ashes of the dot-com bust, launched her consulting practice, and never looked back. In typical Silicon Valley style, Kimberly has helped to start, run, and grow about a dozen small businesses. Several of the startups that she co-founded are still in business and profitable.

Kimberly's clients include companies like Cisco Systems, Symantec, Intuit, HP, Agilent Technologies, Mazda, Daiichi Sankyo, Dow Corning Toray, Mitsubishi Heavy Industries, the University of California, the Institute of Transpersonal Psychology, Siemens, Hitachi, Alcoa, Xerox PARC, NECsoft, NTT DoCoMo, and many more. Nearly six thousand people have viewed the hysterical video documenting the final phase of completing her first book. Have a look at: http://www.youtube.com/watch?v=KDCJBu3rdvk.

Kimberly is contributing to making the world a better place in a number of ways. She's the co-founder of the Open Kilowatt Institute (OKI) and the co-chair of the SDForum Engineering Leadership Special Interest Group (EL SIG). She's supporting micro-finance for entrepreneurs throughout the world via Kiva, and she supports the economic independence of women in various ways because she believes that this is the most effective way raise the quality of life for all people.

Kimberly has been called a "force of nature," a label she embraces. She is obsessed with collaboration, and you can reach "Her Scrappiness" via email at **kimberly@wiefling.com**.

Become a Scrappy Guides Author

Have a "Scrappy" streak in you? Want to write about it? Contact me and let's talk! Email me at **kimberly@wiefling.com**.

Dedication

I dedicate this book to my wife, Julie, who continues to teach me about courage, strength, and what's important in the world (such as problems with flushing the toilet, which her incredible sense of urgency prompted her to point out while I was writing this dedication to her).

To my daughter Bec, whose happy heart never fails to bring a smile to everyone in the room.

To my son Tom, whose drive, laser focus, and determination are bound to have him achieve in life what most could not even dream.

Acknowledgments

Along the journey of my career, there have been innumerable people who have taught, influenced, and directly mentored me in all aspects of business life—and life in general. I gratefully acknowledge the collective wisdom that they have shared with me.

I'd also like to acknowledge—no, I *need* to acknowledge—the eminently scrappy Kimberly Wiefling for giving me the opportunity to write and publish this book. I have never met Kimberly face-to-face (yet) due to our geographically dispersed locations in this globe, but her enthusiasm and encouragement comes through loud and strong with every interaction that we have. Without her support, all of these ideas and thoughts would just be spinning around in my head and would be of no use to anyone (presuming that they are of some use, of course!).

I would also like to acknowledge Mitchell Levy and the Happy About team for their smooth, cheery, and professional publishing service.

For late-night accompaniment while writing, I acknowledge Seal and his album *Seal* (1994, ZTT Records).

Finally, I'd like to acknowledge my parents and grandparents for the values and ethics that they've instilled in me—to always do what is "proper, sensible, and practical."

A Message From Happy About®

Thank you for your purchase of this Scrappy About book, a series from Happy About®. It is available online at: **http://bit.ly/scrappygm** [1] or at other online and physical bookstores.

- Please contact us for quantity discounts at **sales@happyabout.info**.
- If you want to be informed by email of upcoming Happy About® books, please email **bookupdate@happyabout.info**.

Happy About is interested in you if you are an author who would like to submit a non-fiction book proposal or a corporation that would like to have a book written for you. Please contact us by email **editorial@happyabout.info** or phone (1-408-257-3000).

Other Happy About books available include:

- Scrappy Project Management®:
  http://happyabout.info/scrappyabout/project-management.php
- The Business Rule Revolution:
  http://www.happyabout.info/business-rule-revolution.php
- Climbing the Ladder of Business Intelligence:
  http://www.happyabout.info/climbing-ladder.php
- Overcoming Inventoritis:
  http://www.happyabout.com/overcoming-inventoritis.php
- Collaboration 2.0:
  http://happyabout.info/collaboration2.0.php
- 42 Rules for Successful Collaboration:
  http://www.happyabout.info/42rules/successful-collaboration.php
- #LEADERSHIPtweet:
  http://www.happyabout.com/thinkaha/leadershiptweet01.php
- The Successful Introvert:
  http://happyabout.info/thesuccessfulintrovert.php
- Expert Product Management:
  http://www.happyabout.com/expertproductmanagement.php
- Agile Excellence for Product Managers:
  http://www.happyabout.com/agileproductmangers.php
- #QUALITYtweet:
  http://www.happyabout.com/thinkaha/qualitytweet01.php
- 42 Rules of Employee Engagement:
  http://www.happyabout.com/42rules/employee-engagement.php

---

1. www.happyabout.com/scrappyabout/scrappy-general-management.php

Contents

Chapter 1   **Introduction** **1**
- OK, You're in the Big Chair Now............... 2
- Water Skiing—While Everyone Else Is Treading Water............................ 3
- Back to Basics—Keeping It Simple and Sensible (My Version of KISS) 4
- Want to Succeed? Grow a Backbone! 5

Chapter 2   **The Marketplace** **7**
- Understanding the Lay of the Land—Hijack the Google Maps Van........................ 8
- Knowledge of the Crowd or Lunacy of the Herd? 10
- Yes, You Do Still Have to Do a SWOT—and More of Them! 12
- You Know Your Strengths and Weaknesses, so Where's the Opportunity? 15

Chapter 3   **Vision and Strategy—What's the Hallucination for Today?** **17**
- Annual Strategy Session—Too Late! You're Already Dead in the Water 18
- Strategy Shaped by Group Think 20
- Short-Term Objectives (Three Months, or Maybe Three Hours on a Bad Day) 21
- Long-Term Objectives (One to Three Years, if You Should Live That Long) 22
- Painting the Big Picture 23

Chapter 4   **Sales and Marketing—the Job That Everyone Else's Depends On** **25**
- You'd Better Have Good Products or Services, because You Can't Polish a Pile of Poo 27
- Shifting Up a Gear, from Sales to Marketing —Market Orientation 28
- How Does a Market-Oriented Organization Look and Act?............................. 30

The Promise in Your Pitch 33
The Marketing of Services vs. Products. 35
The Use of Services to Repackage Products 35
RFP, RFT, EOI, DUI. 36
The Price Is Right! 37
Partnering—Eliminating a Competitor through
Collaboration 39
The Moment of Truth—Getting the Signature 40
Incumbency—Treasure it! 42
Summary of the Scrappy Sell. 43

Chapter 5 | Production and Delivery—Where the Rubber Meets the Road 45

The Projectized Organization—Coping with
Rapid Change 47
While We're at It, Let's Reduce
Organizational Risk 50
The Project Leader—Internal vs. External
Roles 51
Supply Chain Mangle-ment (Inbound) 53
Keeping Track of Things—What the Hell's
Going On? 54
NPS—Measuring Delight in One
Easy Question 55
Quality and Organizational Culture—the
Human Care Factor 57
ISO Compliance—Is it More Than Just Those
Certificates on the Wall? 58
The Innovation Chestnut 59
Transition Out—It's Going to Happen at
Some Stage 60
Have You Delivered on Your Promise? 60
Summary of Production and Delivery. 61

Chapter 6 | Leading and Developing Your People 63

Do You Really Want to Do Everything Yourself? . . . 64
Recruiting the Right People—Attitude
Over Aptitude 65
Goal Theory of Motivation (Brick-Layer Mentality) . . 66
Three Rules: Communicate, Communicate,
Communicate. 68
Money Is Like Oxygen, Missed When Absent but
Unappreciated When Present 71

Teamwork—Rowing Together to Maximize
Progress 71
Stars of the Future 72
Underperformers—Releasing People to
Their Next Great Adventure 73
Bad Apples—Get the Heck Out! 73
Downsize, Right-Size, Excise, Capsize—
Redundancy, Reduction in Force, and Layoffs 74
Forecasting Staffing Requirements— Employ,
Maintain, or Send on Their Way? 75
Offshoring—Managing For Results 75
Celebrations—Weddings, Parties, Any Reason
at All! 77
Births, Deaths, and Marriages 77
Recipe for Happy, Smiling People 78

Chapter 7 | **Managing Relationships—
External and Internal** **79**

External Relationships—This Is Marketing
as Well 80
We Love Our Customers, but Some Are
Really Difficult 83
Entertainment that Doesn't Get You Sent to Hell ... 84
What the Heck Is Probity? 84
Internal Relationships—Getting the Best
Possible Resources for Your Team
(Without Ripping Someone Else Off!) 84
Don't Compete—Collaborate! And Don't
Collaborate All by Yourself! 85
Relationship Quality—Measuring the
Unmeasurable 87
Relationship Round-Out 88

Chapter 8 | **Managing Yourself** **89**

You Are Being Watched 90
Your Management Style—It's All about
Leadership 94
One More Time—Collaborate, Don't Compete! 95
Help Your Boss Meet Their Targets 96
Balance—No Such Thing, but Give It a Shot! 97
Who's Really Running the Joint? 99
A Few More Basics of the GM Life
—Presentation and Media Skills 100
The Lowdown on Looking after Yourself 101

Chapter 9	**Salute to Supporting Services, Processes, and Structures**	**103**
	Googles and Gadgets	105
	Need an IT Technologist? Hell No! Just Ask a Teenager!.	106
	Security and Backups	107
	Jettison the Computer Room—It's Astronomically Expensive!.	107
	Keeping Track of Your IT Assets	108
	A Desk for Everyone and Everyone's Desk in the Budget	111
	Mind the GAAP, It Can Be Taxing	114
	Collecting the Cash/Paying the Bills and Your Staff.	115
	Ethics—Some People Still Live By Them!	116
	Legal Compliance and Legislation	117
	Knowledge Management—Corralling Your Valuable IP.	118
	Facilities—Parking Spaces and Toilet Cleaning	119
	Clean, Lean, Green, and Not So Mean	122
	OH&S—Caution, Work May Be Hazardous to Your Health!.	123
	The Oldest Web—The Web of Relationships	125
Wrap Up	Wrap Up—Now It's Your Turn to Get Scrappy!	127
Author	About the Author	131
Books	Other Happy About® Books.	133

Figures

Figure 1	Porter's Five Forces Model	13
Figure 2	Sample SWOT	14
Figure 3	Inverting the Triangle	31
Figure 4	Sample Relationship Map (ideally color-coded when you make one yourself)	32
Figure 5	Marketing Pitch Level vs. Actual Capability	34
Figure 6	Typical Functional Organization Chart	47
Figure 7	Projectized Organization Chart	48
Figure 8	Performance Triangle	54
Figure 9	The "Ultimate Question" Response Categories	56
Figure 10	The Cone of Communication	69
Figure 11	Cone of Communication for Customers	81
Figure 12	Competing Within the Organization Smashes the Gears—Collaborating Meshes It All Together!	86
Figure 13	My Profile (left), an Approval and Dependence Style, and the Team's Profile (right) in 1999.	92

Figure 14	By 2007, My Style (left) Has Become More Constructive, as Has the Team's (right). The Change was Correlated With Greatly Improved Business Performance. 93
Figure 15	Your Web of Supporting Services 104
Figure 16	Burt and His "Munro Special" 128

chapter 1
Introduction

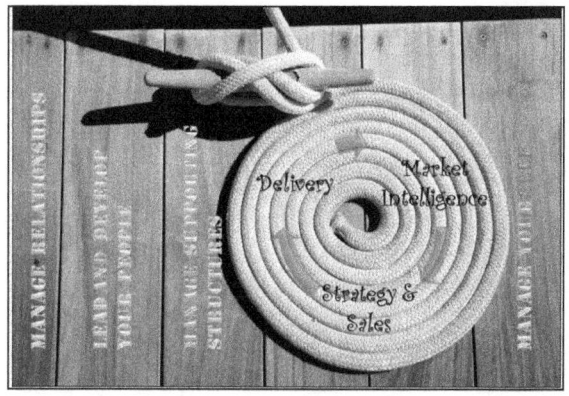

"The person who knows HOW will always have a job. The person who knows WHY will always be his boss."
– *Diane Ravitch, Author, Education Historian*

OK, You're in the Big Chair Now

You've dreamed of this, but now that your dreams have come true your hands may be feeling a little clammy. And while you don't want to admit it, you're feeling a strange mixture of excitement and... well, yes, fear. You're not the leader of a section, or the team of a particular function—you're responsible for the whole shooting match, end to end. You are the business's *general manager* and the people look to you for their livelihoods. Yes, YOU!

So you have to *strategize, sell, supply, and service*; collect the cash, provision, train, and *motivate* your people; delight your clients and, at the end of the day, return a profit to the business owners. So where the hell do you start? And how do you know that you're not neglecting any aspect that will bite you on the bum later? In the moment, that can seem like a heavy load. You may even start to suspect that your success-to-date has been an unlikely string of good luck, a characteristic of the "imposter syndrome," and you may secretly wonder, "Am I up for this?"

Don't stress. It's not all that hard, and it can be an extremely enjoyable and rewarding journey. Whether you're coping in a big company or running a small business, this book can be the ace up your sleeve and will provide you with the common sense and repeatable steps that will enable you to lead, run, and grow a business that everyone will be proud to be associated with. If you're running a small business and there are typical differences from what happens in bigger companies (which will be rare), you'll see Small Business Tips (SBTs) inserted to identify the differences. So, wipe the sweat from your forehead, dry your moist palms on your pant legs, and let's get started!

The font of all knowledge (the Internet) describes a "general manager" as: "The person of general authority who performs all reasonable tasks in conducting the usual and customary business of the principal head or owner" (Answers.com).

Pretty dry stuff, I'll admit, and doesn't give much guidance on how to do any of it. "Reasonable tasks" leaves a lot of room for interpretation, as does "usual and customary." Kind of like describing a kangaroo as a kind of mammal. On my checking around, most commonly, the term general manager (GM) refers to any executive who has overall responsibility for managing both the revenue and cost elements of a company. This is usually referred to as having Profit & Loss (P&L) responsibility. This is the end-to-end role that oversees most, or all, of the organization's marketing and sales functions, as well as the day-to-day operation of the business. Frequently, the GM is also responsible for leading the strategic functions of the company or the division for which they are responsible.

This is the formal explanation, and it is pretty damn close to my understanding of the role, so this is the scope we'll work from for this book. It's going to take a few successes to get that fragrance of confidence surrounding you and nobody wants to follow an anxious and uncertain leader. So lock yourself in the bathroom for a few hours with this book and we'll see if we can give you a jump start to feeling confident in your role as a GM.

Water Skiing—While Everyone Else Is Treading Water

Most people want to achieve success and a comfortable life. So, what is success and a comfortable life from a GM's point of view? You're responsible for the P&L, so clearly, one measure of success is having more "P" than "L." Even if you're a non-profit, that doesn't mean you are running an organization "for loss," so this applies to you, too.

The comfortable part comes from having happy and motivated people that will go out and create that "P" for you. To do that, they'll need to need understand and buy in to the strategic goals and the plan for how to get there, even while they're up to their eyeballs in day-to-day tactical challenges.

When the whole shebang is working well, it's a great feeling—and at times you'll truly feel like both you and your team are water skiing, speeding above an ocean of opportunities, leaving unsatisfied sharks snapping in your wake, while your competitors are struggling to keep their heads above water. But it doesn't happen by magic! It does take some organizing. I'm quite often asked how our management team was able to achieve the results that we've delivered. Usually it's obvious that the person asking is expecting a "bolt of lightning" type of answer. Sorry to disappoint, but there isn't one. The truth is that there is no one thing, or even a dozen things that make the organization hum. It is *many* dozens of things that need constant attention and fine-tuning. If any one of them become out of wack, or ignored, you'll very quickly start to see the negative impact, usually in your monthly financials.

Outside influences obviously can contribute to creating these imbalances, but like a person becomes injured or ill, the healthier the organization is, the better it will cope with the knocks and the quicker it will recover.

Back to Basics—Keeping It Simple and Sensible (My Version of KISS)

The key to long-term, sustainable success is keeping things simple and sensible. Simple means easily understood, easily maintained, easy to spot where the problem areas are, and easily replicated.

"Sensible" is what that little voice in your head tells you will lead to the right outcome. You may have heard the story about the quality certified concrete life jacket—made to perfect ISO specifications. What was missing? Common sense!

How many times have you heard the story about a company selling its goods or services at a price that made you think to yourself, "There is no way they could do it for that price and make a profit; it just doesn't make sense! Well, it didn't! Months, or even years later you hear that the company has gone into bankruptcy, closed down, or been sold. You were right all along—it didn't make sense, and that's why they ran into trouble. Even horrifically bad ideas can work for a while, but eventually the laws of common sense must be obeyed. The airline industry is a classic example, where 97 percent of new airlines fail to last a decade—usually due to their suicidal style of fare discounting.

There isn't a lot of gray area here. When it comes to finances, you either have enough money to invest, or you don't; you either have enough income and collateral to cover a debt, or you don't; and you're either making enough profit, or you're not. It's as simple and sensible as that. Any fancy accounting and finance tricks are just going to be hiding or delaying the inevitable bad news. Some extremely well-known examples of this in the investment industry have proven this point beautifully, with painful results for anyone with even moderate net worth. (Plenty of people in the U.S. have seen their 401k retirement accounts become a 201k as a result.)

When it comes to your staff, colleagues, and customers, you're either doing the right thing by them, or you're not. Nothing complicated here either. And it doesn't matter what YOU think about your leadership or the quality of your customers' experiences. It's what your people and your customers think that counts.

No matter what the scenario, a good test of what's simple and sensible would be to mull over the question: Could I explain this to my dear old grandma, and have her understand it and make sense of it? It might take two cups of tea and a hot buttered scone, but if you could get away with without the "oh gawd, I don't know what you're on about," then you've got a winner!

Want to Succeed? Grow a Backbone!

"Never, never, in nothing great or small, large or petty, never give in except to the convictions of honour and good sense."
– Winston Churchill, speech to the boys at Harrow School, October 29, 1941

Some organizations seem to require the removal of this bit of skeletal structure, but I think it's an essential ingredient for a Scrappy GM. The challenges you face will come from both within and beyond your organization, and in both cases you'll need to have courage and conviction to succeed.

Some of the toughest times will occur when you are battling your own organization about things that don't make sense.

SMALL BUSINESS TIP: This will probably be the owners of the business, maybe even family... even trickier if it's the in-laws!

If it doesn't make sense to your own people, then it's probably not sensible! Naturally, there will be all sorts of personal agendas, oversights, and naivety that will have contributed to the scenario that you are facing. Keep in mind, only in rare cases do people come to work with the malicious aim of intentionally doing a bad job. But that doesn't prevent them from doing stupid things. Your job is to enlighten them to a more sensible approach without striking fear into their hearts, causing long-lasting bad feelings, or having them lose face. Your job is to find the win-win rework of the scenario that's causing the issues.

Externally, the same kinds of headaches will occur, particularly with competitors, suppliers, regulatory bodies, government entities, advisory councils, consultants, and any entity that wants a slice of your pie. Although these external stakeholders may just be doing their job in their own best interest, in this realm people may be maliciously trying to trip you up. Don't have too much faith in humanity when dealing with your competitors! They're out to eat your lunch at the first opportunity. When facing these challenges, we need to take Winston Churchill's advice and never give in, sticking by our ethics and doing what's sensible.

Throughout this book, we'll help you navigate through the mine field of issues that stop most managers in their tracks and have them accept failure or a lower than optimal outcome... this is not the case with a Scrappy GM! But you'll have to supply the backbone! Ready? Let's get busy.

chapter 2
The Marketplace

"I keep six honest serving-men (They taught me all I knew); Their names are What and Why and When and How and Where and Who."
– *Rudyard Kipling, from The Elephant's Child, Just So Stories for Little Children, 1902*

Understanding the Lay of the Land—Hijack the Google Maps Van

While the world around us is full of surprises, everything that we do in managing a business is cyclic and repeated. But even in a continuous cycle, there is a natural starting point, and I think the logical place for the business management cycle is in understanding the market that you are operating in. At the very minimum, you need to understand your position in the market, your competitors, and your customers. If you manage to do a good job of this, you can then identify your target market segment, define what it is that you're actually going to sell, and then make sure that you can sell it at a profit.

Early on in my career, I had no real idea how to gain this understanding. Sitting at my desk wondering what the hell to do, I commented to my PA about my dilemma. Her pearl of wisdom was, "I think you should go out for lunch." I'm not sure if she understood how powerful what she had said was, but what a bloody great idea it turned out to be! I went out for lunch for two weeks straight, entertaining anyone who was hungry and willing be entertained, friend or competitor. It was the best path to understanding my local market, IT services, and outsourcing that I could ever imagine. The old cliché of "who's in bed with whom" was becoming clearer with each lunch discussion. I was also able to take advantage of being the new kid on the block, as people always love to give advice and opinions, and I loved to listen to them.

But you can't go out for lunch forever, as eventually you run short of lunch buddies, the expense report starts to put on weight—and so do you (I had to take up running every morning). Eventually I had to start putting my newfound wisdom to use. We've all learned painfully in recent times that the pace of change has increased substantially and that pace continues to increase. Companies fail, new competitors show up, exchange rates shift dramatically over night. Information can change hands so damn quick that it can take your breath away. Wouldn't it be great to have a Google Maps van metaphorically driving up and down your business' "streets" 24-7, taking 3D pictures of what the market landscape looks like, and have it loaded into an information repository that could be viewed and recalled at any point in time or from any point of interest? Well, most of us don't have that luxury, so you need to make as much use as possible of the resources available to you as you can.

You need to know what happened last Friday, in the format that suits you, and the only way you're going to get that information is to get off your arse and get out there—both on the street and with your people. At the end of the day, those with the most up-to-date information of their market are going be best positioned to exploit that information and expose the opportunities before their competitors do.

We could go out and pay consultants to do this for you... but my view is that their work is likely to give you data that can be several months old. It's also likely that a consultant's report will have a flavor that matches their own personal slant. (I know they have a code of practice to follow, but people are people. We're all victims of our own personal biases.) Plus, they're likely to be spruiking the same sermon to your competitors. So where's the advantage in that? Besides, the real value in such research is, well, DOING it. In saying this, though, consultants may be of some use, particularly if you are targeting a neatly defined part of the market and you need some historic data to hook into the trends.

Let's wrap some structure around this "understanding the lay of the land." There are three main categories of market research (an adjusted version of "Information Collection" from Millier and Palmer):[2]

- Exploratory research (gathering data from your staff, colleagues, and clients)
- Descriptive research (e.g., using consultants for a defined research topic)
- Casual research (going out for lunch or coffee)

Naturally, you're busy with your day-to-day activities, what with checking email every thirty seconds and all. But let's see how you can attend to these three areas still get some sleep at night.

---

2. Paul Millier and Roger Palmer, *Nuts, Bolts and Magnetrons: A Practical Guide for Industrial Marketers* (New York: John Wiley & Sons, 2000).

Knowledge of the Crowd or Lunacy of the Herd?

On January 28, 1986, the Space Shuttle Challenger was launched at 11:38 a.m. on the six-day STS-51-L Mission. During the first three seconds of liftoff, the O-rings in the shuttle's right-hand solid rocket booster (SRB) failed. As a result, hot gases with temperatures above 5,000 °F (2,760 °C) leaked out of the booster, vaporized the O-rings, and damaged the SRB's joints, causing tragedy.

The first announcement of the event came across the Dow Jones News Wire at 11:47 a.m. EST. By noon, the stock values of the four companies involved in building the shuttle had begun to fall. By 12:36 p.m., the stock market had clearly singled out one company as being at fault, by which time their stock had dropped 6 percent from the pre-crash value. Later studies on stock market trading at the time established that there was no evidence of insider trading.[3]

It was not until six months later that the cause was officially known and published, confirming what the stock market had established in less than one hour. How the hell did the market get it so right, so quickly? It will have been from the many thousands of people all gaining little snippets of information and collectively piecing it all together until the correct conclusion was arrived at—the knowledge of the crowd. James Surowiecki in his book *Wisdom of Crowds*[4] talks about this phenomenon and how seemingly self-interested people can coordinate and cooperate en masse to solve a problem.

Our challenge is to harness this powerful knowledge engine that exists everywhere, including within our own organizations and social networks. I believe the secret to doing this lies in answering the question, "What's in it for me?" In the example of the Challenger scenario, the "what's in it for me" was individuals looking to avoid a financial hit by gathering information from wherever they could and taking quick action based on that new knowledge.

---

3. Michael Maloney and J.Harold Muherin, "The Complexity of Price Discovery in an Efficient Market: The Stock Market Reaction to the Challenger Crash," *Journal of Corporate Finance* 9 (2003): 453.
4. James Surowiecki, *The Wisdom of Crowds: Why the Many Are Smarter than the Few and How Collective Wisdom Shapes Business, Economies, Societies and Nations* (Doubleday, 2004).

A Scrappy GM, who must continually gain up-to-date market knowledge, needs to establish incentives within our cultures that will assure the channeling of market knowledge in a way that it can be effectively used. You can enable this by assuring that everyone in your organization can see the goal and can see and understand the individual and organizational benefit of seeking out and sharing market knowledge. You want to incent them to come forward and contribute their information and insights—quickly, regularly, and positively—understanding the collective advantage in doing this.

You can now effectively collect the market information, but how can you tell that it's not rubbish? Well there's a Golden Rule on market intelligence:

- Information received from one source should be considered interesting gossip.
- That same information ferreted out from two different sources is something worth being considered.
- If you receive the same information from three sources, you probably now have something approaching data.

SCRAPPY TIP: Watch out! The Golden Rule on market intel is known by many, so your competitors may use it to their advantage—by planting misinformation into the market at multiple points. (I know this, as we've done it ourselves.)

How you store your treasure trove of market data depends entirely on what tools you use within your organization. It doesn't matter whether it's a spiral-backed notebook, or a sophisticated software package, as long as the data is up to date, shared, and used. Some sort of framework needs to be established within each organization that ensures a regular scan of the market data and to review for gaps. Ideally this will be part of a weekly sales and strategy meeting—yes weekly, not monthly—just like car dealers do.

A Scrappy GM also needs to maintain the greet-and-eat "lunches" and informal coffee and conversation meetings. It's a good idea to establish a pattern and calendar of all your key contacts within the client base, both existing and target customers, so that you can make sure they are all getting some attention (not just your favorite ones). Mix it up a bit by also having your managers meet with these people, rather than just yourself. And don't forget the cold call, particularly on your competitor's clients! You'd be surprised what some people will do for a free meal. You have nothing to lose.

The last consideration is to make sure that you aren't just following the lunacy of the herd nose-to-butt, only to end up charging off the cliff with the rest. If your competitors are industriously heading off in a certain direction, it doesn't necessarily mean that you should as well. Our "fence at the edge of the cliff" is the market forces studies and SWOT (strengths, weaknesses, opportunities, and threats) analysis, which we will cover next.

Yes, You Do Still Have to Do a SWOT—and More of Them!

Now that you've gathered market intelligence data, it's time to partner that with a SWOT analysis, which will effectively create some decision-supporting information. First things first though. For clarity of thought, before completing your SWOT, do a review of the market forces. This is a great way to aggregate that up-to-date market data that you gathered, and make sure that it's not a load of hogwash. This is most effectively done by applying management guru Michael Porter's Fives Forces Model, shown in Figure 1. And don't feel like an MBA geek either. This model is marvellously simple to create, understand, and discuss—plus it fits cleanly on a PowerPoint slide for sharing with your people. And it really helps organize and visualize the team's thoughts.

Porter's Five Forces Model describes the five forces at play in a market as being:

- Threat of cheeky new competitors in your market
- Threat of buyers themselves doing something crazy
- Threat of substitutes, gawd forbid

- Threat of supply chain "manglement"
- Threat of ever-toughening market competition

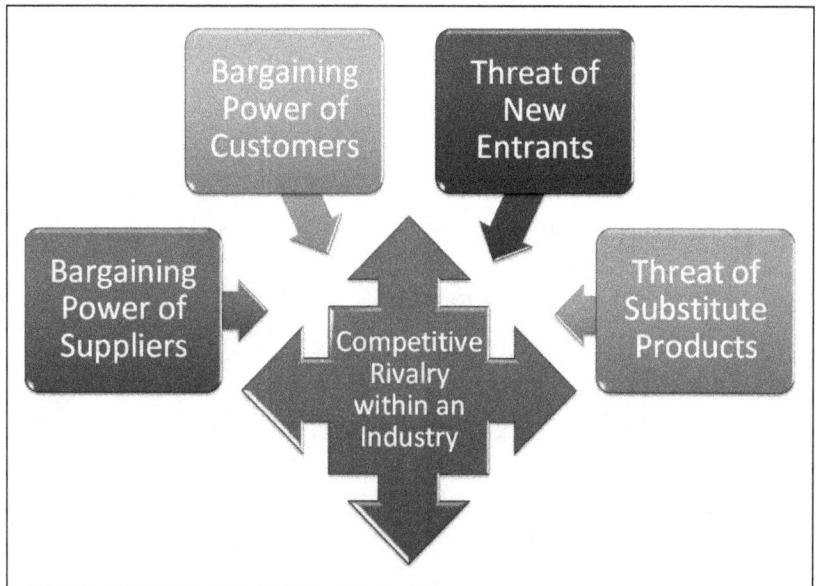

Figure 1: Porter's Five Forces Model[5]

So what we're looking for here is not just a pretty diagram. You're on the hunt for opportunities that can be exploited and strengths that can be built upon, while making sure that you're not going to be blindsided by any threats that may come thundering down the business highway while you're happily tootling across it.

Now that you've collected the market data and studied the market forces at hand, you're ready to start by listing out and studying your strengths, weaknesses, opportunities, and threats—better known as your SWOT (Figure 2).

---

5. http://en.wikipedia.org/wiki/Porter_five_forces_analysis.

Example SWOT Analysis

	The Good Bits	The Not So Good Bits
Looking Internally	**Strengths** 1. Been in business a long time 2. Economies of scale 3. Good customer references 4. Strong balance sheet	**Weaknesses** 1. Lack of flexibility 2. Corporate overheads 3. Outward appearance as being expensive
Looking Externally	**Opportunities** 1. Local market growth 2. Customers perception of cost savings available 3. Merger or Acquisition	**Threats** 1. Government policy change 2. Fierce local competition 3. New entrants encouraged into the market

Figure 2: Sample SWOT

Honesty is required with your SWOT—no spin doctoring. You'll only be cheating yourself. You want to know the 'warts and all' story. The more people that you seek feedback from the better, as everyone will have a slightly different line of sight, and these differing viewpoints will help build the 3D picture that you're looking for.

When redoing your SWOT, one thing that I've found is that it's best to start listing things again from scratch, otherwise the previous listing will throw you off the track and you'll end up with "same old, same old."

Don't even look at the old SWOT until you've done the new one. Then afterwards, when you compare the old with the new, there are likely to be some surprising new developments.

You Know Your Strengths and Weaknesses, so Where's the Opportunity?

The whole reason for the previous analysis is to support you in leading your business toward opportunity and away from disaster. If you're fortunate, new opportunities will be jumping off the page, getting you and the team all fired up. Sometimes it's a case of reconfirming your existing successful sales strategy, encouraging you to stay the course. But other times you'll be staring into a pool of mediocrity, wondering where the opportunities are hiding.

There are a few ways to help flush out the opportunities:

1. Benchmark successful businesses in your area and compare those results to your SWOT.
2. Look outside of your industry for businesses where you can get ideas from that can be applied to your business (like the car companies learning to do faster failure- and root-cause analysis by studying how the U.S. Center for Disease Control finds the cause of public illness outbreaks).[6]
3. Gathering a diverse group of stakeholders and doing a review for previously overlooked possibilities.

The truly scrappy ideas, though—the real game changers, the ones that will let you break from the pack—are going to come out of your own head. This way you can be sure you're not just doing what every other Joe Blow has been doing.

If the opportunities are still not yet shining through, try completing a SWOT on your competitors. Sometimes seeing your business through their eyes can open yours. Another tack is to work through these

---

6. Gregory L White, *GM Takes Tips from CDC To Debug It's Fleet of Cars*, (*Wall Street Journal*, April 8, 1999) http://www.rbbi.com/desks/cs/disease.htm.

exercises directly with your customers. Nothing beats directly talking and listening to customers. Directly asking them what it is that they want won't give you all the answers, but it's a great start! It sounds so simple to say that we should be sitting down with them, and jointly working through our strengths and weaknesses, but it's so often omitted. When you do take the time, don't be surprised if you end up surprised.

If you've done all that and there's still nothing obvious, it's time to consider if what you are trying to do is viable. Maybe it's time to pull the plug. It's better to have this moment of truth now rather than commit time, money, and resources to marketing something that you and the team cannot get excited about. Even though everyone knows that sunk costs should be ignored in business decisions, in reality it's much harder to pull out after months and millions have been spent.

But suppose you're lucky, or good, or both, and there are opportunities. Next it's time to sit down with your team and set or reset your strategy, design your products and services, and get selling!

chapter 3
Vision and Strategy—What's the Hallucination for Today?

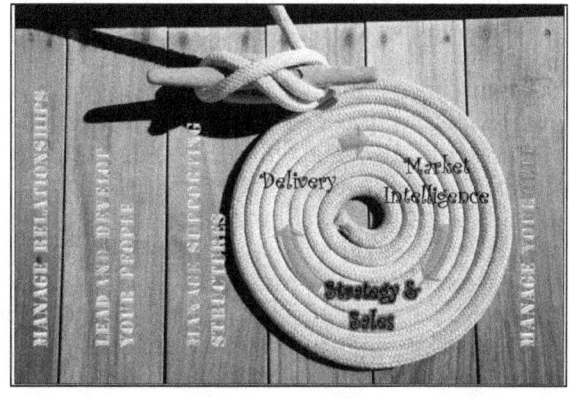

"I can't change the direction of the wind, but I can adjust my sails to always reach my destination."
– *Jimmy Dean (American country music singer, actor, television host, businessman)*

Goals and strategy go hand in hand. Strategy is our roadmap, and it needs to be real, relevant, and readily identifiable—definitely not a hallucination from a few fatigued minds. Operating an organization without a strategy is like taking a journey without knowing the destination or in which direction to head. It may be an adventure, but not necessarily a pleasant or profitable one. And, at the very least, you need a set of goals that are the journey's end point. Your strategy is your road map to reaching those goals. There's no use in having one without the other. You might end up someplace nice, but only by luck, and you don't need a GM for that.

At the most basic level, your goal is to run a profitable business, with the precise measure of success being articulated in dollar terms. Even "not for profit" organizations will need to work to a cost budget figure that is their goal. To achieve this bare minimum there are numerous areas that you need to attend to, such as client satisfaction, quality, compliance recruiting, retention, and dozens of others that we could list, but that just might make us faint before we even start the task. We'll talk more about these and organizational goals in the chapter on production and delivery.

Strategy is an interesting thing, as it is all about self-control, overcoming natural instincts to jump at every opportunity that pops up or to take retributive action if things don't go your way. It's like playing Monopoly, where at the start of the game, you're cashed up and excited, wanting to buy every property you land on. After a while, the cash starts running short and survival triggers your analytical thinking to start assessing how the market is looking. Strategy begins forming, passing up on buying opportunities, looking for that strategic "Park Lane." That sort of self-control needs to be in the thinking from the start of the game. It then becomes a business of "What are the odds?" vs. "What's lucky?," and we're all about increasing the odds.

Annual Strategy Session—Too Late! You're Already Dead in the Water

In times past, this was an annual exercise that usually coincided with the budget cycle. Tradition was that such planning and strategy sessions were done at the start of the new financial year, usually at an appealing location away from the office. These off-sites were usually followed by communication sessions by the born-again managers with the staff about the strategic plan that they cooked up for the year. Once the enthusiasm wore off, the hard copy wound up in a fancy binder and the soft copy was filed in that "Strategic Plans" folder under "My Documents" as everyone got back to doing whatever they were doing a month earlier.

So what's changed? The speed of change. Sure many companies still need require the annual dog and pony show, but strategy is something that needs to be reviewed monthly, if not weekly, and thought about daily. Markets shift dramatically (music CDs to online downloads), markets disappear (film-based photography to digital), and new markets are created (automotive satellite navigation systems). Things are changing that quickly now. Global events used to take months or even years for the effect to trickle down to where changes impacted most businesses, but now the effects of some key events show up in your market easily within a matter of days, or even hours—like when oil prices change, driving the cost of raw materials up rapidly and eroding profits; or when suddenly China is using up the world's supply of steel, causing shortages in other industries; or when other raw materials are in short supply and they are on allocation to the businesses that are competing for them; or when a natural or man-made event suddenly changes the landscape, like an election, a legal change, or an international change. You need to be equipped to respond and keep ahead of the curve.

Focusing on a strategy of reducing costs? Let me offer an opinion—cost cutting alone is not a strategy. It is a short-term, caretaker management style that results in unconstructive behaviours and adverse reactions. Long-term deployment of this management style (which I refuse to acknowledge as a strategy) will guarantee the very lackluster results that all businesses aspire to avoid... and don't you even dare think about tarting it up under a label, such as "Six Sigma" or "Lean Methodologies." Anyone can make their numbers today by milking tomorrow's profits. If you must adopt cost cutting to make your numbers, make sure that it's very short-term. And put a milestone into the calendar to STOP, reconsider what the hell's going on, and start the business analysis process all over again, as something must have failed further back in the chain to get you into this pickle in the first place.

Strategy Shaped by Group Think

I feel strongly that strategizing is best done as open dialogue among your team, and that many people's ideas are likely to be much better than just your own. The additional benefit is that you're likely to get the team's buy in to the strategy. In your capacity as the GM you need to make sure that you don't railroad the discussion one way or another with the weight of your position—not an easy task. Everyone needs to have an equal hearing, and it's often the quiet ones that will be holding the most valuable pearls of wisdom. As long as you can coax them to contribute their wisdom, and presuming you're not unduly intimidating, and your people aren't disproportionately timid, there's no need to have the discussion facilitated. (Still, people with positional power do tend to overestimate how approachable they are and underestimate the fear factor, especially in a down economy.)

Since you should be aiming to review and adjust this strategy regularly, at very short intervals, you don't need to aim for perfection. Your job is to ensure that the end goal(s) are clear and understood. What you're after is a strategy that is simple, sensible, and precise, made up of no more than a few high-level activities, with a couple of sub-activities.

As mentioned previously, you cannot blindly carry out this strategy for the entire year, without occasional review. The whole idea of having a strategy is that it should drive behaviors, decision-making, and resource allocation. In order to assure that this is indeed the case strategy review is best done on a regular basis, perhaps even weekly. Due to this regularity, the format of the review needs to be free-flowing-informal, if that fits—so that adjustments can be made rapidly and easily where necessary. You need to be able to quickly capitalize on opportunities and take action against threats as they arise. Severe market shifts can occur literally overnight, in almost all kinds of businesses and markets. You need to know about shifts that impact you as soon as they happen and proactively respond. If your strategy is simple, sensible, and easily understood, adjustments can be made as a matter of course.

The deployment of your strategy is the link between how to get there and actually getting there. If you want to get technical, the deployment of strategy can be described as a process known as *hoshin kanri*,[7] which has been taken from Japanese business practices and means "pointing direction."

To deploy your strategy, you need to set yourself some short-term objectives that complement and build towards your longer-term strategic objectives.

Short-Term Objectives (Three Months, or Maybe Three Hours on a Bad Day)

This is your "what should we do now" tactical plan—for the next ninety days. It's normally a mix of normal day-to-day activities for running the business, and items that feed into your longer-term plans. It doesn't matter if this is written up formally or informally for the team, scratched out on the back of a napkin or chalked on the factory floor, listed as action items on an internal wiki or tracked as an activity list on a shared document. So long as your people know what they are supposed to do, and they do it. As always, regular communication is the key. It's simple, but not easy.

There are absolutely going to be times when you'll be fighting fires (thus, the three-hour reference). Enjoy the challenges these bring! After all, they do break up the monotony of smooth sailing and easy profits. But don't let such distractions extend from hours into days or weeks. If this starts to happen, then a resolution to find the maniac starting the fires and put a stop to it needs to become part of your short-term objectives.

Here is an example of short-term objectives that I've used successfully in the past. In order to meet this year's financial objectives, there are short-term tasks that must be completed. These also address weaknesses highlighted in the SWOT analysis for our organization:

---

7. James R. Evans and William M. Lindsay, *The Management and Control of Quality, Sixth Edition* (Thomson South-Western, Australia, 2005), 225.

- Recruit a marketing professional to work on new opportunities, plus a contractor to assist during times of peak workload.
- Refresh account plans for the existing clients.
- Establish opportunity plans for new clients.
- Review, plan, and establish appropriate alliances with local organizations.
- Establish regular reviews point for the marketing, account and opportunity plans.
- Communicate the strategic plan to the staff, foster engagement with the plan and a marketing culture. This will be done via an all-employees presentation, followed by the strategic planning document being made available on the company's shared internal Web site.

SCRAPPY TIP: There are times when you and the team have no clue as to what short-term action is best to take. In a quirky sort of way, I've found it helps to refer to The Art of War by Sun Tzu (Google it) for some ideas about how to tackle whatever you're up against. I love Chapter 13, "Use of Spies," so that you can gather more information that may help identify an effective course of action... It's time to take someone out to lunch again and see if you can loosen some lips!

Long-Term Objectives (One to Three Years, if You Should Live That Long)

OK, finally. We made it to long-term objectives. This is where your traditional annual strategic plan is going to feel right at home. But it needs to be referred to and updated regularly, not hidden away like some great-grandparents' wedding photos. I'd suggest a monthly check-up and a quarterly cycle of formal reviews and updates. For larger organizations, the plan will sprout sub-plans, assigned to a division, team, or account team. These sub-plans also need regular reviews, updates, and communication—otherwise, what's the use in having them? Sure it seems obvious, but the most amazingly obvious things are forgotten when people get busy. Your job is to make sure you team does what makes sense no matter what kind of distractions they're dealing with. Once again, simple is good. Below is an example.

> Our strategic objectives will build on the work done during financial year 20xx.
>
> - Achieve an ongoing 10 percent growth in revenue over last year.
> - Improve the profit margin by two percentage points each year for the next three years.
> - Find opportunities to expand the use of our intellectual property internationally, assisting our partners in other regions, while improving the revenue stream for our local organization (this has the added benefit of creating further career opportunities for our people).
> - Become recognized for achievement in our field of expertise.
> - Remain an employer of choice nationally.
> - Further leverage best practices from the global community.

Painting the Big Picture

Strategy isn't meant to be a secret. I'm frequently surprised to find that many people working at non-executive levels in their companies have no idea what their company's strategy is or where to find it. Strategy means nothing at all if it is not communicated.

The best way to get the message across to the larger team is to communicate your long-term plan as the big picture, and then color it in with details of the short-term tactical plan. Finally, bring absolute clarity and sharpness to the picture with specific and numeric targets that will allow each individual and teams to set and track their progress against clear goals.

Below is an example of the kind of goals that bring clarity and relevance to the strategy for a team.

Our goals to support our strategy are:

- *Achieve $55 million or more annual revenue from existing accounts.*
- *Achieve 18 percent or more direct contribution margin.*
- *Days cash outstanding < 35 days, averaged across the client base.*
- *Win one new implementation project-annual value > $2 million in Fiscal Year 20xx.*
- *Win 1 large and strategic new customer-annual value > $4 million in Fiscal Year 20xx.*
- *Maintain a staff voluntary attrition rate < 10 percent.*

Now that you've got your strategy sorted out and communicated, it's time for the fun part-selling!

chapter

4 Sales and Marketing—the Job That Everyone Else's Depends On

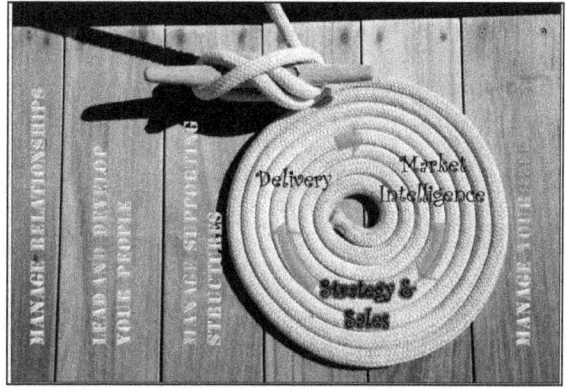

"Now we understand that the most important thing we do is market the product. We've come around to saying that Nike is a marketing-oriented company, and the product is our most important marketing tool."
– *Phil Knight, CEO Nike*

"The spider looks for a merchant that doesn't advertise so he can spin a web across his door and lead a life of undisturbed peace!"
– *Mark Twain*

It's a certainty that not much is going to happen in your business, or any business for that matter, until something is sold. While all aspects of running your business are important, failure to sell will eventually mean that you no longer have a business to run. Calamities occur in the delivery of products and services and you can still make an effective recovery, but selling is what fuels your business, and, if you don't sell, it will splutter to a halt soon enough. The two quotes from the two wise gentlemen above perfectly position a business leader's thinking for sales and marketing. Success is not an accident.

If you've done the background work well and have the right product or service for your target market, this is going to be great fun. If not, you're in for a rough stretch of road. Of all the aspects of being a GM, selling is the area that gives me personally the biggest buzz, and has become almost an addiction. It's also a bit schizophrenic, with my mood swinging from high to low almost day to day according to the latest rumor of whether or not we've closed our latest deal. One thing's for sure, I've never seen a team celebrate with as much conviction as when they've just gotten a good contract win under their belts. And for your business, there's no better addiction for a team to have.

Until I worked as a GM, I had never actually sold anything (except for fundraiser chocolates). I'd ploughed through plenty of textbook theory, but certainly nothing that had brought in a single dollar, yen, or rupee. My first deal popped up after only a few weeks on the job. The opportunity found me, kicked off by the customers themselves. They were unhappy with their current services provider and we had a good reputation and a previous relationship. Although the deal was worth tens of millions of dollars, a very small team, meeting regularly in a coffee shop, transacted it. We negotiated over the fragrant house brew and poached eggs on toast until we'd reached mutual agreement. In fact, the initial sales agreement was done so quickly and cheaply that my own organization initially didn't believe it was real. They even did a check on the signing authority of the fellow who gave me the letter of intent, perhaps fearing that somehow I'd gotten the signature of one of the janitorial staff, and then assigned a senior sales guy to help me close the deal. And close the deal we did—we brought the lawyers into the same cozy little coffee shop, and they also enjoyed poached eggs on toast while the commercial negotiations were done. It certainly was a pleasant and light-hearted introduction for me into the business of selling, and nutritious too.

The key learning for me was that a good quality service (or product) coupled with good relationships, create a winning combination. So how do you go about getting these two elements in place?

You'd Better Have Good Products or Services, because You Can't Polish a Pile of Poo

Having a product or service that your potential customers find appealing is your first requirement. But before you launch into your sales and marketing campaign, go back to basics and review what it is that you're about to go out and peddle.

If you're poised to promote something that you're not proud of, things are going to be unnecessarily difficult. It might build character, but it won't build revenue. If you know in your heart that this is the case—STOP! That's right, come to a screeching halt and reconsider what you're doing. The top priority is to fix whatever the issues are with the service or product. If you go ahead and try "polishing the poo" to make sales, it can quickly catch up with you... in a smelly way. ("Can someone please open a window in here?!") Sure, hiccups occur and a bit of air freshener will be required every now and then in every business. But rushing headlong past this obstacle into the sales process falls into the same category as management by cost cutting—it's a short-term strategy and success will fade quickly if it becomes a habit.

Referenceable customers are as precious as a place to sit at a trade show. Information travels so bloody fast these days that one Internet search can make or break a deal before you even know of its existence. (Over half of all products fail to meet the expectations of customers.)[8] So even in the midst of time-to-market pressures, it's usually well worth it to take a bit of time and fix any major flaws that may lurk in your product or service before unleashing it on the world. However, there are some exceptions, such as when Google releases

---

8. Aberdeen Group, "Making the Case for Collaborative Product Commerce" (July, 2001).

a beta version of one of their applications, or companies target the early adopter crowd in the hope of involving adventurous users in their final tweaking of the product or service.

When we've taken the time to ensure our service is top notch, it's paid off doubly, because the customers have recognized and appreciated the superior quality and have paid us back in continued loyalty and increased business.

What if your services are good, but the client's impressions aren't? Then it's time to bring in the spin masters. Crank up your marketing, use lobbyists, place media articles, and perhaps even wage a positive messages campaign via your employees from all across the organization.

At the end of the day, a good, reference-ready product or service is really only a seat at the table of your market's competitive banquet. Next you've got to work out how to best load your plate and not spill food everywhere or leave anything behind. Get in and have a feast—make a real pig of yourself!

Shifting Up a Gear, from Sales to Marketing—Market Orientation

Now that you have a good quality product or service to sell, the other side of the coin is to make sure you have the best structured organization to facilitate sales success. One that's focused in the right direction—with as many of your resources facing the customer as possible, that will cultivate those all-important relationships. And just like your people are the most effective vehicle for gathering market data, they're also a powerful sales force working for good (or evil) in every customer interaction. Every time one of your people touches a client, they are either increasing or decreasing the chances that the client will be a repeat customer. Organizing your people to be client-facing is known as "Market Orientation," as opposed to "Sales Orientation,"[9] where your customer relationships and customer

---

9. Christian Gronroos, *Service Management and Marketing: Customer Management in Service Competition, Third Edition*, (John Wiley & Sons, 2007), Chapter 13.

knowledge are placed at the center of its business operations. In using a market orientation, you'll have a better chance of producing recognizable value for your customers, which in turn leads quite naturally to more performance worth celebrating. The best part is that this praiseworthy performance is sustainable due to the repeat and ongoing business resulting from having customers that are delighted with your flexible and proactive responsiveness to their needs.

There are three main components of market orientation:

- Customer focus—attentive, responsive, flexible
- Competitor focus—keeping an eye on the market and competitors
- Cross-functional coordination—working as one team in the clients' eyes

So why bother with a market orientation? Shouldn't we just sell, sell, sell? Nope! A market orientation is cheaper in the long run, and increases your chances of winning new business as well as retaining current customers. Studies have confirmed a link between market orientation and improved profitability.[10] The greater the market orientation, the greater the overall organizational performance.

The challenge with market orientation is that it requires an outward focus, but for most organizations the natural focus tends to be inward, tracking for internal gossip, rather than watching the client or the market. This kind of tunnel vision has spelled doom for many companies that lost track of what mattered to their customers.

Perhaps people feel more comfortable looking inward. Maybe it seems safer. But gazing incessantly inward is hazardous to your business health. Make haste and change this *tout de suite*! To change this way of thinking your organization will probably need a cultural shift. Cultural change is difficult at best, costly, and can take years (two or three if you're lucky) in large organizations. For cultural change to be successful, it requires strong leadership (a Scrappy GM is a good start!), who understands the current culture, the new culture, why

---

10. Sabri Erdil, Oya Erdil, and Halit Keskin, "The Relationships between Market Orientation, Firm Innovativeness and Innovation Performance," *Journal of Global Business and Technology* 1, no. 1 (Spring 2005), http://www.gbata.com/jgbat.html#publi.

change is necessary, and how it will benefit the business, employees, and their customers. In addition, the leadership needs to be able to communicate it authentically, with enthusiasm. Once the journey has begun, the enthusiasm will be infectious and one day you'll look around and realize, "Hey! All of a sudden everyone is a salesperson!"

How Does a Market-Oriented Organization Look and Act?

Your business needs to "face" the market in every sense of the word. This could require some structural changes, or, at the very least, a change in attitude. Ideally, it's a flatter structure with more client-facing employees. A flatter structure enables employees at all levels to carry out their tasks without having to refer decisions up the hierarchy. Sensible processes need to be in place. Customer intimacy, which sounds erotic, but is as wholesome as rye bread, has to be infused throughout the culture. People at all levels need to understand that regardless of functional area or job title, they are first and foremost part of a marketing organization. To make this happen, you'll need intrinsic and extrinsic motivation supporting that concept (i.e., ways to help people enjoy working this way and incentives for them to do so). What we're talking about is turning the traditional relationship between the customer and the organization upside down—"Inverting the Triangle" as shown in Figure 3.[11]

---

11. Christian Gronroos, *Service Management and Marketing: Customer Management in Service Competition, Third Edition* (John Wiley & Sons, 2007).

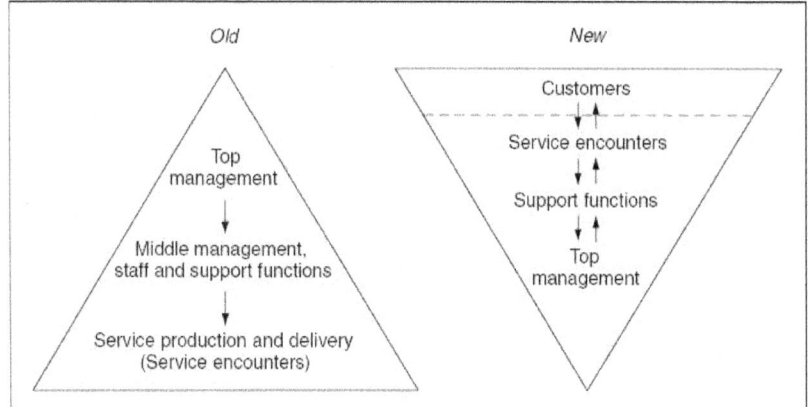

Figure 3: Inverting the Triangle

In this approach, your team must create relationships at all levels of your customer's organization, making use of all available touch points. The planning and tracking of these relationships is most easily accomplished by matching up key people in the customer's organization chart with those in your own. We create a relationship map like that in Figure 4, and use a color-coding system for each person: green meaning that a positive relationship is in place and the person is an advocate, yellow for a developing relationship; and red for when we need to get off our butts and get busy building or repairing the relationship.

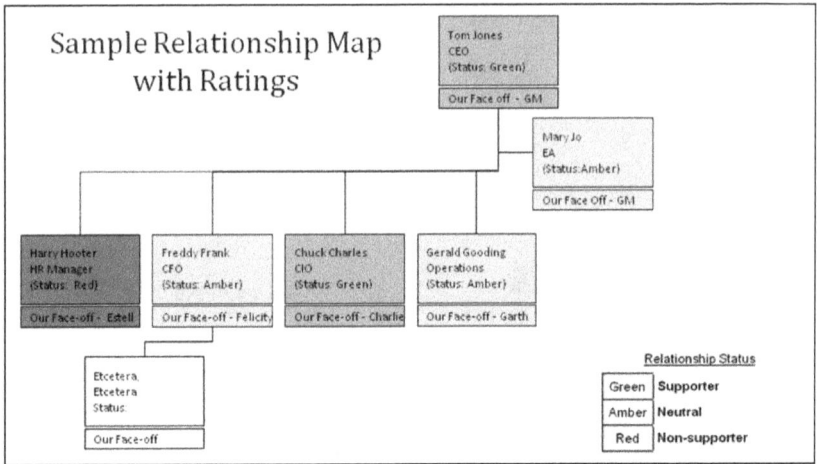

Figure 4: Sample Relationship Map (ideally color-coded when you make one yourself)

Making the shift towards market orientation will also facilitate proactive marketing, rather than waiting for requests to come from the clients. You'll be faster to respond to any requests with more customer-intimate knowledge than your competitors. Additionally, the richness of the communication resulting from these relationships formed will provide insights that will improve the quality of future sales proposals, giving you another jump on the competition.

For our organization, which is based on a matrix structure, the move to market orientation meant shifting the structure from horizontal, internally-focused lines of service to client-facing verticals. The internal focus had been placed there intentionally and was a legacy from the drive for globalization-of-process best practices. But now that this was largely in place, the focus had to return to the client. At first this shift was largely symbolic, but in time the organizational power (meaning where budget was allocated!) also shifted, cementing our market orientation.

The whole point of this change is to enable relationship selling, which is likely to be a less expensive and more successful approach. There is still a place for traditional marketing techniques, but in a supporting role. Your marketing support tool kit bag should be made up of the following spanners and screwdrivers:

- Social media, online (Web sites, wikis, portals, webinars, videos, blogs, Twitter)
- Brochures
- Books and white papers
- Informational and social events
- Lobbyists
- Media articles
- Your people

Social media in particular is shaping up as being a powerful marketing tool—it can be targeted and knows no geographic boundaries, making the world literally your oyster. This one's the new power driver with extra the attachment bits for your marketing tool kit (the ones that make you do that macho *grrrrrr* noise when you hold them... even though you have no idea how to use the bloody things). You'll notice that email and "spam marketing" aren't included in the list above. Scrappy GMs are better than that!

The Promise in Your Pitch

At what level of "promise" should you be making your pitch? There are three choices:

1. Market above your organization's capability (polishing what can't be polished).
2. Market equal to your capability (least risky choice).
3. Market below your capability (undersell, over-deliver).

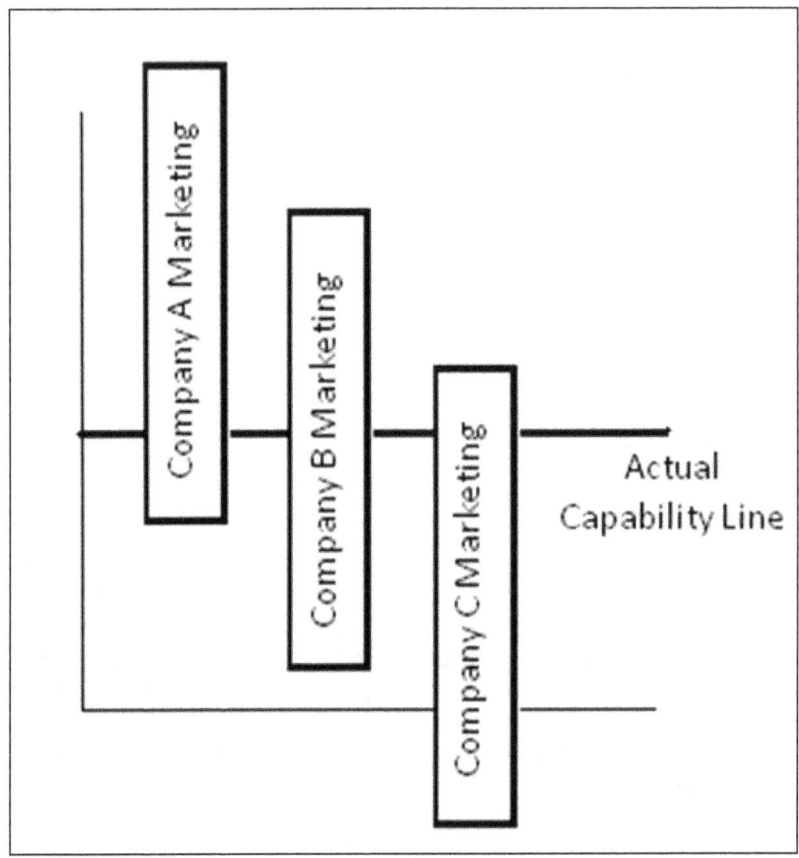

Figure 5: Marketing Pitch Level vs. Actual Capability

The second choice is the least risky because you won't disappoint customers by over-promising something you can't deliver, and you won't lose deals by under-promising what you can. The timeline of success for these three levels tends to run from short term to long term, with the first being a "take the money and run" strategy, and marketing below your capability being the long-term option. The last one, if you can afford it, is tried and true and will guarantee long-term customer satisfaction. This was the well known mantra that IBM used to great effect in times past.

The Marketing of Services vs. Products

A fascinating factoid came to my attention in a book by Laurie Young[12] (an internationally recognized specialist in the marketing and selling of services) where he cites a 2007 U.N. report indicating that services now account for around 75 percent of GNP in developed economies. As countries develop, their economies historically move from being product-based to providing services. We've seen this in the U.K. two centuries ago, again earlier last century in North America, and most recently in Japan. It's likely that we'll see this pattern repeated in China and India as well. In fact India is already taking the lead with their massive offshoring service industries. Similarly, in times past, marketing was done almost entirely around products, with the marketing of services being a special case. The marketing of services is clearly no longer a special case and builds on the experience and practices of the product marketing. In some industries where products and services are bundled together, the revenue from services can exceed that from products by many times, making the importance of service marketing blindingly obvious. People pay for a mobile phone once (if they pay for it all), but they pay for the service month after month, oftentimes for one or more years.

The Use of Services to Repackage Products

Increased competition and commoditization eventually squeeze profit margins on most products. The marketeers are desperate to find any differentiator. In seeking a competitive advantage, organizations often surround their products with services to make them more attractive. An example in the IT industry is Help Desk services provided free to purchasers of PCs. Car companies offer free roadside assistance with new vehicles. It's even become difficult now to purchase a mobile phone that is unencumbered by some sort of "service."

---

12. Laurie Young, *From Products to Services: Insights and Experiences from Companies which Have Embraced the Service Economy* (John Wiley & Sons, 2008).

While marketing of services is fundamentally the same as marketing of products, differentiation can be more difficult with services. Image and quality are important; therefore, successful services vendors are more likely to be market oriented than sales oriented, with customer intimacy being a key differentiator.

When you boil it all down, with services making up 75 percent of mature markets and the larger percentage of the remaining 25 percent now being repackaged under services, in most organizations these days, what we are clearly needing to focus on is the marketing and selling of services.

RFP, RFT, EOI, DUI

When you're selling a service, what you're really doing is selling a promise, and that promise has to be described in a manner that appeals to your customer. This description is your sales proposal. Each customer is unique; therefore, each proposal must also be unique. Do not treat the creation of your proposal as if it were just another project. Otherwise the result will be a "turn the handle" cloned document with all sorts of "oopsies" in it, for example, wrong customer names from cut-and-paste errors. This can be very embarrassing when it's fed back to you during a review of why you lost the deal. It's also embarrassing when a customer points out that pictures you've used in an effort to personalize the document are actually pictures of their competitor's people and equipment. If you want something that truly stands out, treat your sales proposal as an individual, just as your prospective customer will want to be treated.

Proposal themes can be created to mirror the strengths you identified in your SWOT analysis. Take time up front to create themes that are personalized and directly applicable to that particular customer. These themes should be visible and repeated throughout the proposal. You'll also need an elevator speech prepared for each opportunity that reflects what your key themes are. Ensure that everyone on the team knows that elevator speech. Eventually you'll want the client repeating that elevator speech. When they're doing so, you'll know that you are thundering down the home stretch with your competitors squarely in the rearview mirror.

Presenting your sales proposal is often best done by the very people who will be delivering the service. They may not have the polished presentation skills, and are likely to show a few warts, but I'm always surprised about how readily the customers receive this as a more credible story. When your potential customers see the passion in the people, they can quickly turn from being skeptics and critics to being a coach. You can almost see them wanting to put an arm around your people and give them a hug. When this happens, you've won them over, and it's now time to set the right price.

SCRAPPY TIP: Small is good if you want your sales proposal to be sitting on your key buyer's desk. Make sure it's compact and good looking enough to sit neatly in the In Tray or actually on the desk, e.g. thirty pages maximum, with a catchy picture on the front, and a nice folder, preferably pleasant to the touch. This way, it's easy to pick up while they're chatting on the phone if they get asked something and need a quick answer.

A big, cumbersome file is only going to end up stuck in a cupboard or in a box somewhere, only to be read under sufferance at formal review time. Remember, some poor bastard has to actually read this thing. Imagine the fright when a document for review is wheeled in on a fridge trolley! We've done it to a few unfortunate customers and were awarded the outcome we deserved. (Don't call us, we'll call you!)

The Price Is Right!

What price to submit in your proposal? This is obviously the topic that creates the most discussion. The tricky part, always, is deciding the tipping point. At what point is the price cheap enough to win the deal, but not too cheap as to be bad business. Most organizations will have profit-margin thresholds, or hurdle points for pricing, with some sort of governance around making sure that these are met. However, there's always the argument that "this one's strategic" and, therefore, the submission should be a special case and allow lower margins. The problem is that everyone says this to justify lower pricing in an effort to increase the likelihood of winning the deal. If you are extremely lucky (luck which you've no doubt worked very hard for) you'll know the customer's target price or budget, but this is rare. Naturally you have to consider competitive pricing, your costs, and the value of your offering to the prospective client, but the harsh reality is that there is no magic answer here. Rustle up a good portion of debate, throw in a portion of compromise, and then let your educated gut-feel win out.

In addition to what price to set, there's the choice of how to structure your charges—open book, closed book, fixed price, incentive payments, at-risk components, volume-based pricing, cost-plus-fixed fee. There are plenty of choose from. The most important choice, though, is the degree of transparency of your charges that you reveal to your client, and that will depend greatly on the kind of relationship you have. There's a saying that "there's margin in mystery," but, in my experience, if you head down that path there will also be substantial risk, particularly on fixed-price engagements. So, unless you are in the envious position to be able to use "value-based pricing"[13] (where you price according to what you believe the customers are willing to pay), then open-book, cost-plus pricing is the least-risk option for all parties. And, over a long-term engagement, if the relationship is based on sensible grounds, it will definitely help you maintain a win-win pricing structure through times of volatile markets. If the engagement is project based, then the same cost-plus structure can be worked out using milestone payments, so that the customer has some feeling of comfort with progress and control over payment.

How much to spend on your proposal? This is another strongly debated area. Tendering, particularly for large and complex pieces of business is expensive. While you're trying to put a lid on the cost of each sales pursuit, your sales team will be doing their best to Frisbee that same lid out the window at the first opportunity. I've seen guidelines for bid budgets of around 2 percent of total contract value (TCV), and more recently things have skinnied down to 1 percent of TCV. Personally, I aim for 0.5 percent of TCV or even less (now THAT'S Scrappy!). My experience is that spending more money does not equate to a better win ratio. A lower-bid budget will also help discourage people from "adding the padding." Your money could be

---

13. Reed Holden and Mark Burton, *Pricing with Confidence: 10 Ways to Stop Leaving Money on the Table* (John Wiley & Sons, 2008), Rule Nine.

better spent further back in the marketing process on the cultural change activities needed to achieve market orientation. This way you'll spend once and win many times.

SCRAPPY TIP: If you're not being coached by the client on the deal, then it's really only a shot in the dark, and you've just entered a race to the bottom—to the cheapest price. If tender time is your first interaction with the prospective customer, the welcome mat will be out, but the trap door is just one step behind it.

The textbooks tell us this, our clients tell us this, we've experienced it, but like drunken gamblers, we continue to roll the dice to lose money on another cold bid.

Partnering—Eliminating a Competitor through Collaboration

Partnering is a great way to mitigate some of the threats and weaknesses that you may have identified in your SWOT analysis. The combined ability of two or more organizations is frequently stronger than just going it alone. Teaming up will immediately mean that you have access to a wider range of skills and knowledge, have another set of eyes and ears on the street, and someone to share the costs and risks with while you gang up on the market. Partnering works particularly well if you need specialist skills that your organization doesn't have. The added advantage of partnering within your local market is that you immediately eliminate a competitor, and, although you'll have to share the revenue, that's got to be better than getting none at all.

One downside when partnering, however, is what to do with the "margin on margin" situation. Clearly both organizations will be looking to make a profit, and the customer usually only wants to deal with one entity, so you'll probably end up with one organization acting as a prime and one as a subcontractor. If both are looking for a cut, you now have a "margin on margin" situation, and therefore might be likely to price yourself into an uncompetitive situation. Solutions usually involve reducing margin—or creating an alliance-based organizational entity. However, there are plenty of good examples of where using someone else's contract, such as a subcontractor's, do deliver positive outcomes for the client. In many cases this expedites the process and saves the costs of having to advertise, tender and negotiate a new contract in order to get the work started. These savings will often outweigh any pass-through margins that the prime contractor may have to apply to the transaction.

Longer-term strategic alliances make sense when the partnering organization and your organization complement each other well on more than just one client opportunity. If this is the case, a longer-term strategic alliance can be formed, with contractual frameworks that can evolve with each new business opportunity. Although not as risky and messy as a merger, alliances can be tricky, and cultural factors must be considered. The most robust alliances occur when the partners have similar cultural characteristics. And, as in all human relationships, trust is the all-important factor in enabling mutually beneficial behaviors that lead to desirable business results.

There are times when opportunities to partner with organizations that have dissimilar cultural characteristics to your own pop up. Don't discount them out of hand. Sometimes that old saying of "keep your friends close and your enemies closer" may be an appropriate strategy. Just sleep with one eye open.

The Moment of Truth—Getting the Signature

A dilemma that you may face as a GM is the question of whether you should assign a professional sales person to an opportunity—or have the people who are going to deliver the service or product carry out the sales activity. At the end of the day, it depends on your customer. You clearly need to remain flexible to the customer's likes and dislikes. One size does not fit all, and you run the risk of annoying the very people you are trying to impress by not allowing flexibility in your sales approach.

When engaging a professional sales person (or anyone involved in selling, really) there's the age-old theory that there's nothing like a chunky commission to focus a sales person's efforts... and it's bloody right! The "what's in it for me" (WIIFM) has to be alive and kicking for someone to get off their backsides and make the effort to make the sale. Any sales person worth their salt usually has a healthy WIIFM radar. A clear and unambiguous discussion about the personal gain in the deal for them will invigorate their efforts to push a sale across the line. Even small rewards can be extremely motivating.

Before getting a signature, you'll need to get the contract negotiations out of the way. Whatever you do, don't let a room full of your lawyers and their lawyers have a meeting! I've found it's a good idea to actually sit in with your legal people and their legal people during this time, just to make sure things don't start to drift. The WIIFM perspective of our legal colleagues can sometimes make things a little more complicated and drawn out than they perhaps need to be. Their job is to minimize risk on both sides of the equation. The least risky deal is no deal, so you can see how their motives might not totally align with yours. Your job is to get to a signature. Your presence can help encourage things to stay on track and focused on closing the negotiations.

SCRAPPY TIP: If negotiations aren't tracking well and it's looking like you'll never get to an agreement and contract, look for other alternatives, such as subcontracting via an incumbent supplier or any other mechanism that will get the engagement under way—your contract, their contract, some else's contract, some fly-by-night contract you downloaded from the Internet (or, maybe not)—pretty much anything to start work and get the revenue flowing.

"Time kills all deals" is a saying that a sales training guy at our firm constantly repeats. What a great saying to have rattling around in your head as the final part of the sales cycle starts to drag out. Repeating it to yourself and your team can act as a reminder to make sure that sitting around and waiting is part of the strategy, and light a fire under people to prevent the "I've run out of energy on this one" attitude. Silence can be death on the deal. So if there's no heartbeat, it's time to get out the paddles, charge to 180 volts, and give things a damn good shock. The electric shock may come in the form of offering a different finance arrangements, discount for more volume or longer-term contract—anything that re-energizes the discussions.

If the team has done their utmost and it still looks like the deal has gone off the rails—due to price, delivery hiccups, personality conflicts, whatever—never give up! (Winston Churchill again.) As the Scrappy GM, you're the last line of defense against losing the deal, and if you've done the work and have the relationships in place, dig deeper, grow a stronger backbone, and get in there and apply whatever voodoo or hypnosis on the customer that's needed. Whatever you need to do to pull it over the line (barring anything prohibited by law of the land, the Geneva Convention, or anything that would prevent you from entering Heaven)… do it! You've haven't lost until someone else is signed up—and even then you can take it back off them if they slip up.

SCRAPPY TIP: There will come a time when you know the deal is won. When that happens, shut up!—because the next person who speaks loses. Never sell past the close!

And when you come back to sign the contract, as soon as the signings are done and the back slapping is finished, get the hell out of there!—before buyer's remorse kicks in.

When success is finally in the bag, celebrate with those in your company who made it happen. In addition, thank everyone involved at the client as well. Make sure it's special! The celebration dinner should be expensive, polite, and include a few heartfelt speeches.

Incumbency—Treasure it!

Incumbency is to be treasured, as it gives you such obvious advantages, providing you aren't polishing the unpolishable. Love your client, deliver excellence, and you'll be rewarded, either by not having to compete for the business again, or by having the inside track well before the contract expires. Remember that with a current client you have the relationships, the IP, and the added advantage of no transition costs. But don't sit on your laurels or your backside, as taking it easy is not a valid strategy—ever. We've done it and the outcome was a cold bucket of water in the face. The business went elsewhere and we were left realizing that we'd done too little, too late. Never again! It was too painful admitting to our employees that we'd lost the business. Losing when you've done your best is one thing, but losing when you could have done better is much worse. Having to do the walk of shame in front of your people, well that positively sucks.

So wherever possible you need to grab the chance to proactively improve your competitive offering. Contract renewal without having to compete in the open market is a gift, for all involved. Usually over the period of a contract, efficiencies will have been created, whether it's in delivering a service or creating a product, and things should have improved. This is the time to recognize these efficiencies and bring them to the table as a pricing discussion—offering to either do the same for less or more for the same. It may eat into your ongoing revenue totals, but not nearly as much as the risk of having to re-compete the business on the open market. There's also the opportunity to discuss increasing your scope of work—and revenue. So do what you can to create the opportunity of a non-competitive renewal.

Summary of the Scrappy Sell

- Ensure you have the appropriate quality services and products you need before you start marketing.
- Create a market-oriented attitude and organization to facilitate relationship-based selling.
- Use traditional marketing as a support mechanism—especially in the area of social media.
- Keep your sales proposal short and sharp.
- When it comes to the close, never give up!

chapter 5
Production and Delivery—Where the Rubber Meets the Road

"Promises are the uniquely human way of ordering the future, making it predictable and reliable to the extent that this is humanly possible."
– *Hannah Arendt, German Political Theorist*

You've analyzed, strategized, marketed, and sold. The contracts and the expectations are in place, so now it's time to get down and dirty—and deliver on your promises. This is part of the day-to-day running of the business that is one of the key activities for a GM, but that doesn't need to mean it takes up all of your time. Setting up the right structures, processes, and controls will allow things to run smoothly and predictably without your minute-by-minute micromanagement.

When you first step into a new contract, there's a transitional piece of work to get all of this in place. Depending on its size, this is likely to be a sizeable project in its own right. This project should be no different than any other style of project that your organization undertakes. You need the same goal clarity, detailed planning, governance activities, and execution excellence. Some of the likely activities for this project are the familiarization and training of your people, setting up the physical environments required, implementing the necessary tools and processes, establishing the supply chains (inbound and outbound), and setting in place contract governance and reporting measures.

This transition period is an important time for any contract. "Don't judge a book by its cover" is a common enough saying, but guess what?—we often do! Your customers will judge you by their first experiences with your team in the execution phase. So, when kicking off the initial activities, this is the time more than ever that you need to put your best people and best practices to work. A well-executed transition will build trust, save you and your client money, reinforce the customer view that they've made the right choice, and go a long way towards cementing the positive relationships you've created during the contract negotiations. Don't be surprised if there are a few bumps at the start anyway. It's been said that "real boats rock." There'll be a few rocky moments as new interactions, processes, and practices are put in place. And most teams experience the well-known cycle of Forming-Storming-Norming-Performing[14] as early relationships are established. But with your best people on the job, there'll be less storming and more performing in the mix.

---

14. B. Tuckman as cited in Jack Ferraro, *The Strategic Project Leader: Mastering Service-Based Project Leadership* (Auerbach Publications, 2008).

The Projectized Organization—Coping with Rapid Change

The rapidly changing business landscape every businessperson is coping with means that one of the key things that clients are looking for is flexibility. In short, we need to be gosh darn GUMBY! (highly flexible cartoon character from the last century). Customers value your flexibility to shrink and grow your delivery to match their changing business needs, or to alter what is being delivered. These rapidly changing requirements can be difficult to deal with in a traditional organization. So what's the best way to organize your teams to enable this flexibility? An effective way for your organization to cope with these constantly changing requirements is to rearrange structures to move away from functional organizations—or, gawd forbid, matrix organizations—to a projectized organization.

What I mean is, if your organization currently looks something like this:

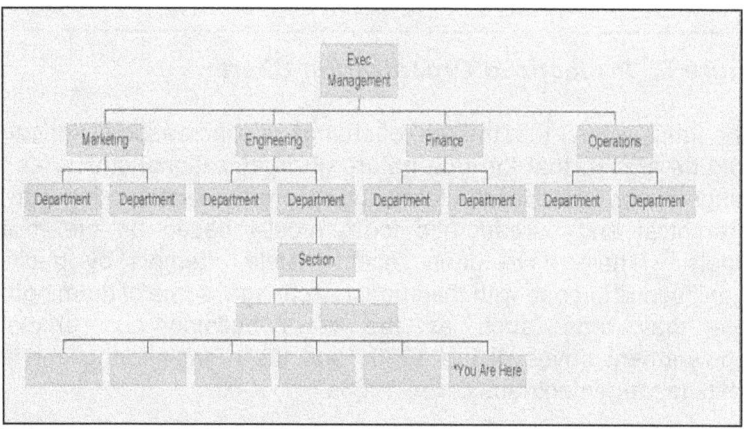

Figure 6: Typical Functional Organization Chart

Change it to something like this:

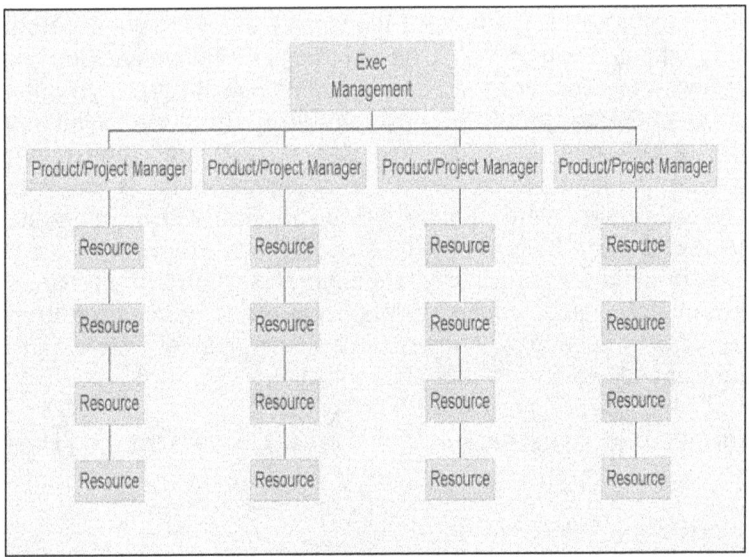

Figure 7: Projectized Organization Chart

Although it is clear that the rate of change has increased historically, it could be argued that the true nature of organizational structures has changed very little over the last century, pretty much sticking with the hierarchical and bureaucratic form, mostly based on the military models.[15] There have been recent visible attempts by business organizations to cope with the impact of change, some of them nothing more than fads, such as the team building and employee empowerment drives of the 1970s and the reengineering and total quality management fads of the 1990s.

Flexibility and responsiveness are a basic requirement these days if you're going to cope with the amount and speed of change. The easiest way to achieve this flexibility is to design your organization so that you can compartmentalize the work into projects—eating the elephant one bite at a time. The key supporting framework, like facilities

---

15. C. Barker and R. Coy, eds., *The Power of Culture: Driving Today's Organisation* (New York: McGraw-Hill, 2004), Chapter 2.

maintenance, electricity, and plumbing, may be permanently in place, but the core business—the work that directly brings in revenue—is done by project teams. A project may be scoped in the traditional sense, or it could be defined by the period of a contract or a production run of a particular product. A nipped-and-tucked, results-centric organization ensures that the people engaged in the work at any time are only those people actually required for the work. That way you're continually ensuring the organization is on a permanent weight loss and fitness program.

Similar to the organizational change required to achieve a market orientation, the move to a projectized organization will require the ever-painful organizational change. Many people will be thrilled to know that their roles, and even possibly their job titles, will change according to whichever way the revenue wind is blowing. These changes may not be in the actual organizational structure, but they will definitely impact the way that the work is carried out on a day-to-day basis. A projectized methodology is also not going to be without its own headaches. An approach is needed to ensure you aren't carrying underutilized staff from a previous project (hangover headache), or a waiting list of people for the next project (stress migraine). The pill to fix this, and the cure for what ails you, will be ongoing resource forecasting, and that means constantly looking up the line at your new business sales pipeline. One "Gumby Organization" actually adjusts their resource requirements and the size of their workforce daily: The ever—Scrappy Kimberly Wiefling[16] explained to me a scenario of one "Gumby Organization" she deals with, that calls their service provider every morning and tells them how many people to send. While most businesses don't need to go to this extreme, a more flexible human resource pool will enable you to better match your staff to the business need.

SMALL BUSINESS TIP: Use of subcontractors and casual labor is a great way to ensure that you aren't carrying "just in case" staff.

---

16. Kimberly Wiefling, *Scrappy Project Management: The 12 Predictable and Avoidable Pitfalls Every Project Faces, Second Edition* (California: Happy About, 2007).

While We're at It, Let's Reduce Organizational Risk

Moving to a projectized style of organization also gives you an opportunity to avoid risk. When the organization is running smoothly, in a "crank the handle" mode with no natural break points in the work, it's easy to overlook risk, even when it's staring you in the face. A projectized structure and mentality creates natural review points in the business flow. Each project decision point is an opportunity to pop your head up and take a look around, spotting any nasty risks lying wait in the bushes and creating your mitigation plan.

Although it might seem a little bit of a sneaky approach, sometimes the best way to avoid risk is to avoid doing the work at all, passing it over to a competitor or subcontractor. Working in a projectized environment enables you to do this, matching projects to the availability of your resources. And, if things are quiet and you're in need of work, you can look at taking on riskier work that you'd normally pass over. With a projectized organization in place, at least you and your management team will have the opportunity to make such decisions consciously, and you'll have a better chance of avoiding the pitfalls in riskier work that you're better off passing by.

Once you're under way with a project or a set of projects, there's nothing like a bit of "Earned Value"[17] monitoring to help keep an eye on things. OK, the mention of earned value tends to make people roll their eyes, look at their watches, and head for the nearest exit. But, properly used, it can be a highly valuable tool for managing a project. If you are among the fortunate group of people who have never heard of earned value, it's a set of measurements that provide an indicator of how your project, and suite of projects, are tracking against budget and schedule. For a mind-numbing review of this topic, please surf the Web. Plan to spend a couple of weeks exploring the topic. For now, let's just say that, if set up well, a single earned value indicator and variation of "plus or minus one" can give a busy GM a very handy and quick read on how things are going on a project, or across the whole business portfolio. A rating of one means that everything is on schedule and tracking to budget. Less than one and there's trouble

---

17. Charles I. Budd and Charlene S. Budd, *A Practical Guide to Earned Value Project Management* (Management Concepts, 2005).

brewing. More than one, fortune is smiling upon you, and you're ahead of the game! The cumulative scores for each project can be added up to give you an overall indicator as to where you stand across a set of projects.

Earned value is no substitute for overall Scrappy General Management, but it's a useful tool, and you should at least understand it before you cast it upon the scrap heap. The whole premise of earned value is to provide an early warning bell that rings if things are heading off the rails, and to give you a quick pointer about where to go and snoop around to find the root cause. It may also help you avoid risk, particularly financial risk, and save you from an unsalvageable situation and an unpleasant demise.

The Project Leader—Internal vs. External Roles

In moving to a projectized organization, there is also need for a renewed focus on how to execute projects with excellence, especially by encouraging project managers (PMs) to adopt an attitude of leadership instead of management. Project management training traditionally concentrates on having people "manage" their projects to an administrative framework. Working strictly to this framework can cause the project manager to take up the habit of navel-gazing, becoming inwardly focused rather than paying attention to the customer and target market. Drawn into the trap of managing and executing to the project plan, and working to achieve the internal deliverables specified in the original project charter and requirements, many a project manager is lulled into a sense that they are actually being successful when they are just ticking off boxes on their own internal checklist.

But what's the problem with that? Isn't that what we want project managers to do, execute to plan and deliver to the requirements? Well yes—and no. What has been emphasised in traditional PM training is the need to concentrate on managing the "triple constraint," another fiction that is often mistaken for reality. But the triple constraint is, once again, taking an internal focus to the project, concentrating on the project dimensions of schedule, scope, and resources. I believe that this myopic view has the potential to stifle any leadership traits. Scrappy Kimberly Wiefling suggests that we should "wave goodbye to the triple constraint," referring to it as "outdated," to put it mildly.[18]

Given that what we are all trying to cope with in our business world is the ever-increasing pace of change, most projects are going to be at risk of having shifting requirements and ever-evolving expectations by the customer, right from the get-go. In this scenario, if your project manager sticks strictly to the original requirements document, then someone is likely to end up at the finish line crying in their beer or getting their butt kicked, or maybe both.

Of course what's really required is to have our project managers trained in project management in the traditional Project Management Institute (PMI)[19] sense. But then they need to keep all of this in their back pockets, using the Project Management Body of Knowledge (PMBOK) as an effective guideline, then lift their heads and look around to see what's happening externally to their projects. An example would be where changes in the customer's management have occurred—and what's important now may no longer match what was important at project initiation time. A widening in the thinking would enable the project managers to deal with the organization and the customer at a business level. This could include project selection or the contracts under which the project would be executed. Their thinking would then shift to a results-driven focus, from a customer view, rather than project methodology driven outcomes.

As anyone who's done it knows, filling the shoes of a project manager is not easy, as one must take on the role of both a leader and a manager in order to succeed. So, rather than retrain a traditional style project manager for a leadership position, we've found that a better solution is to recruit people that already have the natural leadership traits we're after, then equip them with the technical project management skills they need to succeed. The most essential of these skills are:

---

18. Kimberly Wiefling, *Scrappy Project Management: The 12 Predictable and Avoidable Pitfalls Every Project Faces, Second Edition* (California: Happy About, 2007), page 17.
19. Project Management Institute, *A Guide to the Project Management Body of Knowledge (PMBOK® Guide), Third Edition* (Newtown Square, PA: 2004).

- Interpersonal
- Awareness
- Presentation

They're all people skills and they're not rocket science.

Supply Chain Mangle-ment (Inbound)

This is obviously an important area for any business, but in most cases it's a distraction from your core business. Let someone else do it! In other words, the more you can outsource here, the better! The goal is to get as close to "just in time" stock control as possible, to optimize your cash flow. One of the best ways to do this is to not have a warehouse—at all. That way you'll avoid the inevitable collection of crap that will occur wherever a cozy bit of shelf space exists. If you've outsourced everything, including your warehouse, then the monthly invoice from your outsource partner will provide a great "hit you between the eyes" reminder for inventory control.

In choosing your supply chain vendors you will be looking for organizations that will compliment your own. In doing so you'll want to cover some of your own weaknesses, identified in your SWOT analysis. You'll be looking for vendors that can mesh seamlessly with your processes and data systems. They'll need to be certified according to your requirements and have the right cultural fit. Sound familiar? It should be! It's exactly what your customers are looking for when they select you as their vendor. As you design your supply chain, keep in mind Blanchard's advice that you should "keep your friends close and your suppliers closer."[20]

---

20. Dave Blanchard, *Supply Chain Management Best Practices* (John Wiley & Sons, 2007), Chapter 5.

Keeping Track of Things—What the Hell's Going On?

It's obvious that you need to keep your eye on the road when driving in order to avoid an accident. (Reading your email on your iPhone while swerving madly into oncoming traffic, however common, isn't advisable!) Similarly, you need to keep an eye on your business' performance if you're going to avoid a calamity. So what do you need to know? Not much really—just three key measures that must be tracked regularly:

1. Financial performance
2. Customer satisfaction
3. Employee satisfaction

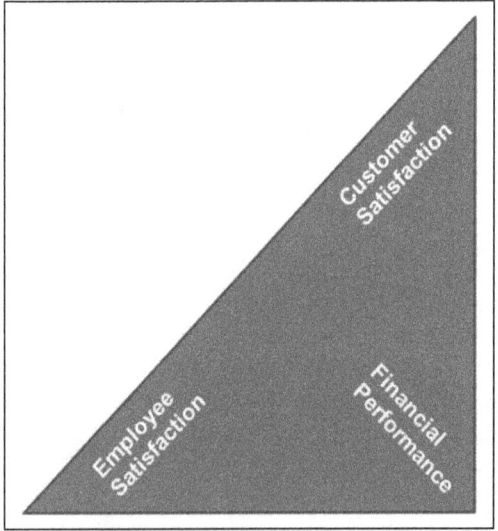

Figure 8: Performance Triangle

In effect, they form an equilateral triangle (see Figure 8). If the length of one of the legs increases, then it's probable that the others will, too, and your business success will also increase. There's no such thing as coincidence in how these three factors interact. You can be sure that all three are inextricably linked, and any imbalance in one is quickly going to be reflected in the other two.

Are there three equally easy measures? As you're probably aware, finances can be quite involved, but the key measures will be to track revenue, profit margin, and cash flow against your targets. The other two, employee satisfaction and customer satisfaction, can be effectively monitored by making use of the Net Promoter Score (NPS) system popularized by the book *The Ultimate Question*, by Fred Reichheld.[21]

NPS—Measuring Delight in One Easy Question

There are innumerable methods of surveying customers and employees, but most are laborious both for the person replying to the survey and for those collating and interpreting the data. So, in the spirit of simple and sensible, there's one question and one question only that needs to be asked—the "Ultimate Question":

"How likely is it that you would recommend our company to friends and colleagues?"

The answer is in the form of a numbered rating in the range of one to ten, with one being loosely interpreted "Never! No way!" and ten being "Absolutely! Sure gonna do it every chance I get!" Depending on the rating received, the answer is grouped into one of three areas—detractors, passives, or advocates—using the Likert scale[22] in Figure 9 below. The fence sitters, or passives, are ignored. Using the totals from the other two groups, a score for "customer advocacy" is calculated based on the percentage of advocates and detractors relative to the total number of advocates and detractors combined. This is known as the Net Promoter Score,[23] or NPS.

---

21. Fred Reichheld, *The Ultimate Question: Driving Good Profits and True Growth* (Harvard Business Press, 2006).
22. http://en.wikipedia.org/wiki/Likert_scale
23. http://en.wikipedia.org/wiki/Net_promoter_score

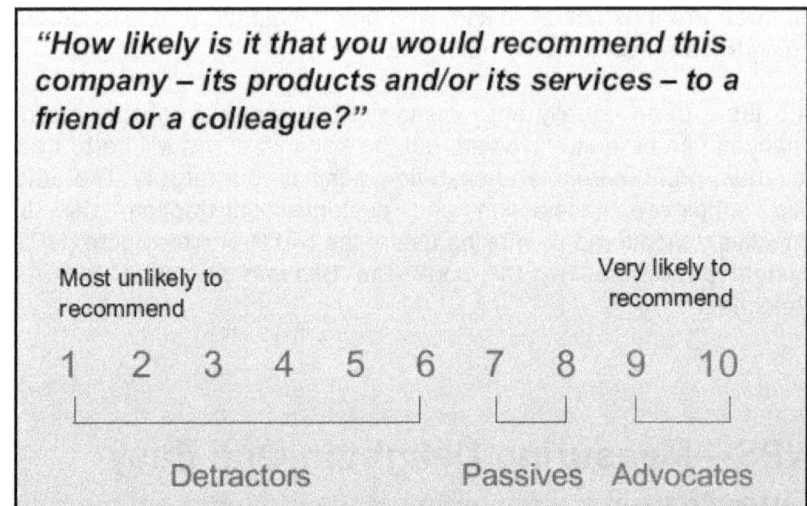

Figure 9: The "Ultimate Question" Response Categories

Net Promoter® Score (NPS) = [% of Advocates] - [% of Detractors]

The trends in this single piece of feedback provide a pulse on customer or employee satisfaction that is easy to understand, even if it masks a plethora of root causes. The numerical results of this survey appear to brutal to the first-time user, but a quick search of the Internet will reveal that those employing global best practices don't score all that high. The percentage is just a number—a figure of merit—not a letter grade in high school. I've found that the results from these surveys can quickly direct you to problem areas or high performing areas very accurately—even if you're unaware of the underlying causes of these areas. In one early survey that we did we had what would be considered a great overall result (33 percent). However, there was one particular customer who rated us quite low relative to the overall score. We'd been delivering according to promised service levels, and had no "off track and in the weeds" projects, so I was puzzled as to why the low rating. I then happened to glance at my schedule of client "catch-up meetings" and noticed that this customer wasn't on the list—anywhere! We hadn't been paying the person that was being surveyed any attention. As soon as I remedied this with a quickly organized lunch, things miraculously turned around and, within weeks, we had a contract renewal in the bag. If it hadn't been for the NPS survey I'd have been none the wiser of this customer's true feelings.

NPS surveys can be carried out simply by email and/or by using one of the online survey services that are readily available. It is equally effective with both customers and employees, and provides a great pulse check on your business health.

SMALL BUSINESS TIP: Even if you only have half a dozen customers, and staff, this simple survey can still provide great feedback. Even more so if you have a person independent of your business ask the question.

Quality and Organizational Culture—the Human Care Factor

What all Scrappy General Managers dream of is having an organization that naturally creates quality services or products as a matter of course, day in, day out, business as usual, without having to rely solely on processes and procedures. To achieve this requires employees for whom quality is second nature. What we're talking about is a pervasive culture of quality, and this is not a concoction you can just add to the office coffee pot.

Creating this kind of quality culture may require cultural change (yes, this topic again!). To make this a reality, there will need to be policies that relate to communication, job design, employee performance, and, maybe most importantly, rewards systems that align with the quality management objectives of the organization. With this cultural change it's entirely possible to spend a boatload of time and money on a quality management program with absolutely no gains. Don't go there! It's a waste of your time and your employees' time.

ISO Compliance—Is it More Than Just Those Certificates on the Wall?

All this quality talk inevitably leads to thoughts about certification. You may be a NASCAR driver, but if you don't have a driver's license, you're breaking the law if you drive on the roads. Similarly, you may have achieved a stunning level of organizational-wide quality but, unless you're certified, in many industries, you won't be trusted to carry out the work. Certification usually comes in the form of testing, registration, and compliance to an ISO (International Organization for Standardization)[24] standard. In order to be considered as a vendor for the companies using certification as a screen, you need to be certified to operate. But, more than that, you need it to operate sensibly. A host of cynics will tell you otherwise, but the ISO only asks you to "say what you do and do what you say," operating your business in a predictable and repeatable way. Those who view the certification process as a paperwork and hoop-jumping exercise miss the point entirely—and most of the benefits.

You must keep in mind that certification alone will not ensure a useful product. What you put forward for certification is entirely up to you. The verification process basically checks that what you say you are going to produce is what is actually produced. Period. The most memorable example I recall from my early ISO training was the "quality-certified concrete life jacket." It passed all the production quality and specification checks perfectly—the problem was, it didn't float! ISO certification doesn't tell you what to make or how to make it. It just confirms that you are performing with some level of consistency and a solid foundation for continuous improvement, as it's tough to improve a chaotic process that's delivering results that are all over the map.

I've heard the debate around quality management being a fad that peaked in the 1980s and early 1990s. For companies that have been successful long term, quality management is clearly not a fad. It's part of the *kaizen* (Japanese for "improvement" or "change for the better") continuous improvement cycle, where tools such as Six Sigma and Lean Methodologies are applied to suit the organization's needs. Even if quality management is or was a fad, each iteration is advancing the global knowledge base of business management. Gibsone & Tesone

---

24. http://www.iso.org/iso/home.htm

explain that "... the content of the fad becomes part of the overall experiential base, which means new fads should be at equal or higher levels than the preceding process."[25] So, fad or not, embrace it! It's working towards the greater good of global management practices.

The Innovation Chestnut

It's difficult to do such an important topic justice here, but, in reality, this is what being Scrappy is all about—being innovative. Have you heard feedback from your clients like, "You're not being innovative enough," or, "Where's the innovation?!" If not, then you're probably not talking with your customers enough. Innovation is one of the biggest buzzwords of the twenty-first century! Unfortunately, I've been through plenty of mediocre innovation brainstorming sessions, customer meetings, and the suggestions box routine. Results can be a bit like the old quality circle style meetings—lots of neat minutes, but not much beyond the "let's print double-sided to save paper" kind of ideas.

Upon reflection, these lackluster results were a result of looking at the issue backwards—looking inwardly for the ideas rather than searching outside, exploring what other organizations in related fields of business are doing. For example, what does an offshore oil and gas producer have in common with a water utility, and what can they learn from each other? Plenty! They both pump stuff around in pipes. The oil and gas company has invested huge amounts of money in managing the tight timeframe requirements for maintenance shutdowns. The water utility has decades of experience in managing aging assets, particularly in areas of corrosion management. One beneficial approach is to bring case studies to your clients about what others are doing in related industries then discover how to apply these ideas to your client's situation.

This is one of the most effective ways to break out of incremental thinking and crack the innovation chestnut. These and other open source approaches to innovation like those discussed in the books

---

25. Jane Whitney Gibson and Dana V. Tesone, "Management Fads: Emergence, Evolution, and Implications for Managers, Academy of Management Executive 15, no. 4 (2001): 122-133.

Crowdsourcing by Jeff Howe and *Wikinomics* by Don Tapscott have delivered results that were previously unattainable, and even unimaginable, using traditional approaches. If you haven't read these books, it's time! Soon you'll be up to your hips in the ideas contained therein.

Transition Out—It's Going to Happen at Some Stage

No matter how successful your business is, there will come a time when your project will come to an end, and you'll have to hand it over to a client employee or, gawd forbid, a competitor. Keep in mind that what goes around comes around, and you never know when it will be time to re-engage with the customer for the next piece of work. So the approach here needs to be exactly the same as when you transitioned in. Aim for "no loose ends." Put your best people on the job, don't hold anything back, and don't leave any "gotchyas" behind. There should be no time bombs ticking when you walk out the door. Transition out with pride, and, before you know it, the customer will be back for more.

Have You Delivered on Your Promise?

How do you think you've been doing? Maybe the monthly report is nicely presented, bound with a plastic cover and a picture conforming to the latest company style guides. However, the big test is not what shows up behind that well-presented cover, in the balanced scorecards, service level agreements (SLA), or transaction reports. Often the best indicator of how it's going is how you feel when you go to meet with the client, the same person or people that you gave your sales pitch to. Do you feel the indicator in the pit of your stomach on high alert, the urge to get in and out quick so that the conversation doesn't have a chance to get past the pleasantries? (I've had that feeling many times, and ventured in with my tap dancing shoes at the ready, hoping to hell that the conversation didn't land squarely on the project overruns or missed delivery dates before the sugar's even been stirred into my coffee.) Or, preferably, is the meeting an occasion you look forward to, where you're comfortable, sitting back, relaxed, and enjoying the meeting, happy to allow the discussion to drift into any area of delivery—past, present, and future?

If the answer is the latter, then it's more than likely that you and the team have delivered on your promises. This is a wonderful feeling for all parties, and the rewards are that repeat and additional business will head your way as a result. The other good thing is that happy customers usually pay their bills on time! It's a double positive whammy—increased or repeat business and improved cash flow.

Summary of Production and Delivery

- Put your best foot forward to enable a successful transition to new projects.
- Deploy a projectized organization for increased flexibility and reduced risk.
- Turn your project managers into project leaders.
- Outsource inbound supply chain.
- Use simple performance metrics, and review them regularly.
- Cultivate a culture of quality and innovation.
- When it's time to transition out, do it with pride and no loose ends.

chapter 6
Leading and Developing Your People

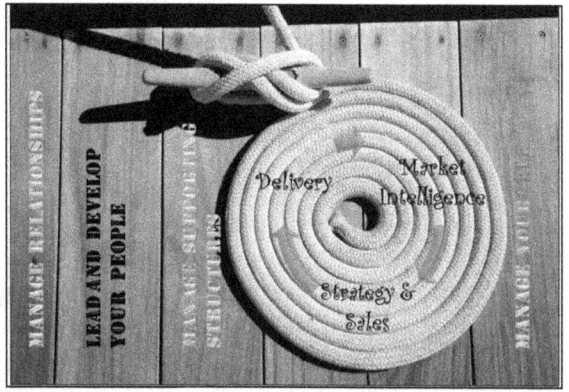

"Leadership: The art of getting someone else to do something you want done because they want to do it."
– *Dwight D. Eisenhower*

Do You Really Want to Do Everything Yourself?

As Scrappy GMs, we're in the people business. The work of real human beings provides your revenue, and your employees provide that work. It's a simple equation, but a delicate one. Your people are obviously everything to your business. Many companies proclaim this via a plaque on the wall or slogans bandied about, but living it is another matter. We've already talked about your people being your vehicle for gathering market information—and for your marketing outreach. They're also your main competitive advantage, the one resource that your competitors cannot readily duplicate... although the cheeky buggers will try to poach your good ones away from you (and sometimes they'll be successful). Therefore, your attention needs to be directed at nurturing, coaching, aligning, focusing, rewarding, and retaining this all—important organizational resource.

There's certainly more to leading your people than just providing a paycheck. (I hope this doesn't come as a terrible shock to anyone reading this, but there are parts of the economically developed world where the word still hasn't gotten out.) They'll require intrinsic motivation, something they bring to the table themselves, inspiring goal setting, and extrinsic motivation via rewards (pay) that are linked back to the goals, and a respectful dose of appreciation every now and then. Teamwork and collaboration are behaviors that you need to encourage through your leadership in order to ensure that your people and their knowledge are turned into tangible business results.

When you've got a great team in place, you want them to stay put. To assure this, your people will need to be coached, developed, and given every opportunity for their personal growth. As unintuitive as it sounds, the more marketable that you can make them, the more likely it is they'll hang around. It's not reverse psychology. It's appealing to the WIIFM (what's in it for me), the radio station that everyone on earth is tuned in to. If they do end up moving on to some other great opportunity, then you can feel proud of their achievements... and it's more than likely that they'll be back some time in the future with even more experience and capability. Some people will be happy to stay in the same job year in and year out, and that's great! Your job is to make sure that they find their special spot in your organization and feel appreciated for what they contribute.

Recruiting the Right People—Attitude Over Aptitude

We all want great employees and I believe the process of selecting them is all about attitude. People with the right attitude are capable of anything with the right training and support. Too often we select people based on technical skills and experience only to find out later that there are some major deficiencies in the attitude department that cannot be corrected. They may be trying really hard, but they just don't seem to be able to hit the mark.

So, what's the right attitude? The key attributes to look for are straightforward: energy, awareness, taking ownership (EAT).

In other words, you're after a self-starter, who's aware of what's going on around them and cares enough to make the challenge at hand their own. With these attributes, and the appropriate technical training, you'll have an employee that will EAT any challenge.

When interviewing prospective employees (or even when I first meet someone casually), I'm terribly impatient and tend to pass quick judgement. It's human nature. People get categorized before they even get a chance to sit down. What they're wearing, how they wear it, how they talk and greet you, body language and eye contact, all influence the opinions others instantly form about us. This is something that all of us instinctively do, and with some degree of accuracy according to Malcom Gladwell's book *Blink*. But you don't want to be too much of a cowboy! You can't just base your hiring decisions on gut feel and first impressions! In order to make good hiring decisions you'll need to make sure that there is some sort of balance brought into the interview process, with a prepared format, a guiding set of questions, and a method of scoring. This is especially important if you are interviewing a number of people. Having one or two others sit in with you is also an excellent way to gather valuable second opinions.

Personally, I pay little attention to the resume other than the basic information, as a shockingly large percentage of resumes contain misrepresentations of the truth, and you never know who's really done the writing and formatting. However, I do check to see that the person has made some kind of a contribution, an indicator of their willingness to take ownership. References are sometimes useful if you can talk to the referees in person, but don't count on getting the truth out of people who may have bad news to deliver. The liability laws in some countries make it too darn dangerous to say anything more negative than, "Yes, we worked together." But if you can get someone to talk with you in person you might be able to detect their true opinion of your prospect's character and work quality. The best situation is if you know and trust the reference, or if you can mine additional references from the original ones so that you are talking with people who were not directly referred to you by your prospective new hire. These folks are least likely to have been prepped by the candidate, and so you have a better chance of getting honest comments from them.

SCRAPPY TIP: If you need to carry out a large number of interviews in a short period of time, names and faces can become a blur. Take a photo of each candidate and file the photo with your interview notes—or even create a visual org chart of the people you've interviewed. (Oh, and make sure you get their agreement first—no spy cams! That's just not cool, and it's certainly not Scrappy!)

Goal Theory of Motivation (Brick-Layer Mentality)

So, you've employed the right people, they have great attitudes and skills to burn, but how do you keep them motivated and wanting to stay with you? Although quaint, hoping that they'll work hard just because they like you is a flawed leadership strategy, so you'd better have a backup plan. Plenty of research and my own personal experience suggest that there needs to be a good mix of extrinsic and intrinsic motivation to keep people performing at their peak. The formal rewards system will go a long way towards providing the extrinsic motivation, but it will need to be linked to, and inspire, the intrinsic motivation within each person via the goal setting process.

Creating an environment that supports the intrinsic motivation in each person is vitally important, particularly in a service organization. In such organizations, you can work your backside off all day long, but when you get up from your desk at night, it's hard to see what's different from when you came in that morning. People in service industries struggle to obtain a sense of achievement. If they can't see what they've done, and they don't know where they're going, it's hard for them to get motivated.

This is where goal theory of motivation comes in. It was developed in 1968 by Edwin Locke and Gary Latham, American psychologists who probably never worked a day of their lives as employees in the business world.[26] Nevertheless, their theory is compelling. I refer to it as the bricklayer mentality. At the end of the working day, the bricklayer can look back and see what they've built, which gives them a great deal of intrinsic satisfaction. They can also visualize what still needs to be done, giving them the motivation to come back the next day. The goal theory process works like this:

- Goals must be set collaboratively, so that everyone feels ownership.
- The goals need to be a stretch, yet achievable. Goals that are too easy or too difficult actually de-motivate people.
- The goals must be specific, and numeric if possible, to remove any ambiguity.
- A progress tracking mechanism must be established that makes visible to everyone feedback on the progress.
- Celebrate success and coach off-track situations.

Once you've jointly set the goals, drive the message home by linking them back to people's rewards, with consequences for missing the mark. Within my own team, many of the goals are financial. I can tell when the goal setting is working well by the amount of banter at the monthly finance reviews. Usually reviews would be as boring as watching paint dry, but when things are working well, suddenly everyone's interested, firing questions at the finance guys as to "what's this figure and that figure." Just the fact that they've turned up to the finance review is an indicator!

---

26. Edwin Locke and Gary Latham, as cited in Marilyn Helms, ed., *Encyclopedia of Management, Fourth Edition* (Gale Group, 2000).

Three Rules: Communicate, Communicate, Communicate

As previously mentioned, you're in the people business, and in the people business you have to communicate—all day, every day. Some people do this well instinctively, with seemingly little effort, while others are all noise and babble, ideas and concepts ricocheting off the walls. Don't leave good communication to chance! You can't afford to leave this part of your leadership strategy to a good luck potshot. These three rules will help you hit the mark every time.

Communication Rule #1: Be Consistent and Persistent

You can have the best-laid plans and strategies in the world, but they will amount to nothing unless they are communicated to someone—to everyone—on your team. Your people are the ones who are going to execute your fabulous plan. The vision needs to be articulated, the targets clearly described, and the "how to" plan explained in detail. And just as strategy is no longer a once-a-year event, communicating the strategy can't be a rare annual event—it needs to be done repeatedly, at every opportunity. Establish an ongoing cycle of communication, with your messages reflecting the latest shift in thinking. If the strategy is a picture on the flat screen, your communication is the pixels that paint that picture and add clarity, and those pixels will continually shift to form the updated picture as the plans are refreshed.

For best results, organize a framework for communication ranging from formal to informal, with the intervals ranging from daily to every six months. This is illustrated in Figure 10, The Cone of Communication.

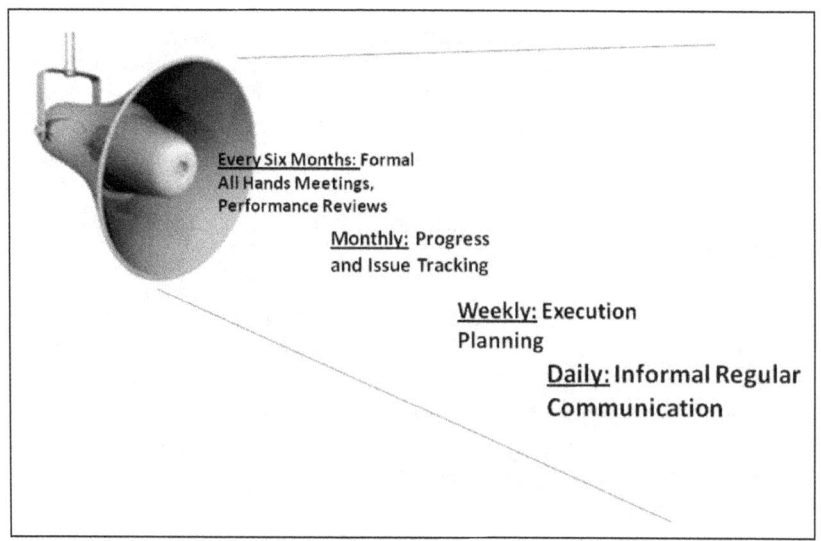

Figure 10: The Cone of Communication

SCRAPPY TIP: Do you want to meet regularly with your management team and have a free-flowing exchange unhampered by bureaucratic minutes and action items?

Something I've found that works really well is to meet briefly each Monday morning and go through everyone's calendar for the week. This triggers all sorts of useful discussion, while still giving a loose framework for sharing what's top of mind for everyone. Works like a charm on getting each other up to date and setting the scene for the week!

Communication Rule #2: Be Positive, Positive, Positive!

At the risk of sounding like a visit to Disneyland, in corridor talk, in meetings, when presenting to your people, the messages must always be positive. Even if the news is bad, smoke up a positive spin. You've always got to be asking, "What does this make possible?" no matter how nasty the presenting symptoms appear. I learned the hard way early on in my career about the reaction that you'll get to negative comments in a presentation (and it wasn't pretty!). Never again was anything even slightly negative ever allowed past my lips in a formal presentation, or included in a slide presentation (PowerPoint should have an automatic "Warning: Negative Content" feature!). Upbeat is the way to go. You don't need to be a pie-in-the-sky dreamer, but at worst, be "realistic." Don't go on record as a negative ninny! There are always possibilities, and it's your job to see them hidden in the piles of poo and communicate those possibilities to your people so that they can figure out how to make it so.

The same message applies with electronic communication (email and Web postings). Always be positive! This is even more important here, as your messages can be reviewed over and over for added impact and effect. So keep all those helpful admonitions to speakers rattling about in your head (e.g., "What's not said, doesn't have to be defended," and, "If in doubt, leave it out.")

Communication Rule #3: Walk the Talk

You can enact the first two rules perfectly, but their impact will amount to nothing if you don't walk the talk. Actions speak louder than words, and your actions will be noticed far more than your words, so they absolutely have to be in line with all of your messaging and communication. A major part of walking the talk is to listen. *Really listen.* Our esteemed editor, Scrappy Kimberly Wiefling, advocates "Generous Listening," but whatever you call it, make sure you do it.

SCRAPPY TIP: If you have people located remotely, regular communication with them is not going to come naturally, so you need to make an effort and find any excuse to ring them up and create an interaction. When I've had large numbers of remote staff, I'd keep a copy of the org chart at my desk and tick off each person's name when I spoke with them, making sure that I spoke with each person regularly and that no one was forgotten. (I often wonder if they caught on to how methodical I was about this. If you know any of my people, please don't tell!)

Money Is Like Oxygen, Missed When Absent but Unappreciated When Present

As we've alluded to in this chapter, keeping your people happy and motivated isn't all about money. There are other factors at play that enhance the positive workplace experience. A major one is the culture and "feel" of the place. Do the employees connect well as colleagues and in teams that work closely together? A strong team bond creates a supportive and constructive environment. You can tell when this is in place by the banter and joking that occurs between team members. There'll also be a willingness to pitch in and help those that are struggling, and backfilling without griping when people are sick or on vacation.

I have also seen great loyalty and performance from employees such as working mothers, who are provided flexible working hours and other seemingly minor benefits such as reserved parking. There's not a lot of cost to the organization in facilitating these kinds of bennies, and the potential for improved employee performance is well worth the minimal risk. Working from home, study leave, and travelling to conferences and trade shows, are other "perks" that are well appreciated, and can improve the quality and quantity of work carried out. It certainly does take a lot more than a hefty paycheck to create the positive work environment needed for long-term performance.

Teamwork—Rowing Together to Maximize Progress

It makes absolute sense that a well-focused team is going to be much more effective than a group of well-intentioned individuals heading off in different directions. Your leadership, strategy, and goal setting are the ingredients needed to get the team all rowing in the same direction—and the right direction.

Diversity in a team is highly desirable. Strength comes in numbers, and that strength is enhanced if each team member is uniquely strong. If a team is diverse in many dimensions—age, gender, culture, education, and beliefs—it then has access to a broader range of ideas and abilities. When recruiting for our team, we aim to attract a person who can bring complementary strengths to what we currently have on board, and also counter any weaknesses that we may have in the team (SWOT thinking again). An underlying principle of my leadership approach is one of acceptance and celebration of these differing styles and personalities, not merely tolerating, but revelling in the color that it brings to the group.

Stars of the Future

Developing people is a highly rewarding part of the job, but there's a helluva lot more to it than just sending people off on training courses. Training is for circus animals. People need professional development. They need to learn how to think, and they need to shape their judgment and hone their skills to operate effectively under high-stress conditions. For my money, coaching and mentoring is the way to go, whether formal or informal. It is a fantastic feeling to mentor people and see them succeed, even if they're not aware that you're consciously doing it. Scads of people have helped me along the way, and I see mentoring others as my way of paying them back. Most large organizations have formal development programs, with a yearly review and performance-plan update. Unfortunately, it's frequently just window dressing. Get serious about it! Pick out someone special and help them along on their career path. If we all did that, even for just one person, the window dressing wouldn't be needed any more. One particular young fellow that I helped contacted me a couple of years back when I was visiting Sydney, and came in to the hotel where I was staying. He was very proud to show off his new wife, new baby, and new car (all three were sparkling and shining) and insisted that none of it would have happened if I hadn't helped his career along earlier in the piece. It was a both a humbling and satisfying experience and, on my part, had taken very little trouble.

Underperformers—Releasing People to Their Next Great Adventure

Sometimes it's time to go. Your people are like parts of a car—they'll need continual maintenance, improvement, or replacement, and some wear out sooner than others. A touch of preventive maintenance can save you a ton of time and money. However, if large repairs are required, it's often easier to replace the faulty part with something new or better engineered than jury-rigging the existing wobbly piece. This can also be the case with people. A person with some minor performance issues is usually worth with the time and effort to bring them up to snuff. However, if the person has major performance issues, then replacement might be the best option. In the long run, that usually works out better for everyone. Few people come to work intent on doing a bad job. Keep this in mind. It is your sacred responsibility to help the ones who are struggling find an alternative that suits them better. That's a lot more compassionate to them than letting them twist in the wind and frequently ends up being a win-win situation for all involved.

Bad Apples—Get the Heck Out!

Sometimes it's *definitely* time to go. There are times when you will have people on your team that are just plain rotten apples. There's no room for fraudulent, corrupt, bullying, or sexual harassment behaviors in a productive work place. These are all "no second chance" scenarios—you need to move these people on as quickly and cleanly as possible. Work with an HR professional to formulate your plan before engaging these short-timers. The HR folks are likely to have a list of "50 ways to leave your lover" that can help you disentangle from the working relationship without ending up in court. Push the boundaries if you need to—you need these people out! If you don't take immediate action, the whole apple barrel will quickly go bad, and your company culture will be tainted by their toxic impact.

Downsize, Right-Size, Excise, Capsize—Redundancy, Reduction in Force, and Layoffs

It happens. The reasons vary, from a sensible reaction to market changes, to the unfortunate result of mismanagement. It doesn't matter how you got here, you're here, so deal with it. When you can see the writing on the wall (and you will know, or at least you should!), be proactive. Like a tsunami, workforce reduction programs destroy everything in their path. Take the high ground early so that you can manage the layoffs for your business from a position of integrity. Hiding and denial will only mean that you get swept under with the rest of the flotsam and jetsam.

Layoffs are never a positive experience, and it's the kind of scenario that halts culture in its tracks. The downsizing is best done quickly and with as little fuss as possible, while lending as much compassion and support as you can to the affected human beings. During this time you need to be very visible and approachable, but watch out that you don't get drawn into justifying the need for the layoffs. It is what it is, simple as that. Your team's reaction will be predictably unpredictable, so cut them some slack and don't get tangled up in the emotional drama. Everyone deals with stressful situations differently. This will also be a very stressful time for your HR people, so keep an eye on them as their brave faces often hide their real thoughts and deep emotional concerns. They, like everyone else, will need someone to talk to (and HR people are usually good talkers). As for yourself, try to not dwell too deeply on the agony of the situation or you'll put your head in the paper cutter and do yourself in.

No matter how nervous or badly you are feeling about what you need to do, remember that it's much worse for the person sitting across from you. Do whatever you can to make this experience as dignified and painless as possible.

Forecasting Staffing Requirements—Employ, Maintain, or Send on Their Way?

The aim of forecasting what size staff you'll need is to make sure that your people are neither idle nor overworked. Let's revisit a couple of concepts that we have already discussed that link to how you manage and forecast your staffing requirements:

For future growth: The fact that your management teams are engaged and active in the sales and marketing cycle will also mean that they have visibility to the pipeline of work that is likely to be heading their way. This, coupled with the existing work requirements, should give them and yourself a view as to what is required.

For the existing workload: The projectized work environment makes forecasting easier. The project view enables a look at the resources required across a program of work, identifying opportunities for leverage where possible. Resource leveling that can be carried out in the projectized environment also helps maximize the effective use of your people. As long as you're not woefully under-resourced, you don't have to have as precise of a crystal ball. You can move resources around from one project to the other to assure that the highest priority jobs get done.

Offshoring—Managing For Results

If your business is sizeable, it's more than likely that some portion of your business will be done from locations remote to your main headquarters. If this is the case, you'll be expecting similar performance from your remotely located people as you get from those located just outside your office door. The same rules apply to remote staff as to your local people—you'll need to recruit for attitude, and they'll need to be equally, even if culturally differently, motivated. They will also need consistent and regular communication, just like the people at the home office.

There are, however, some additional aspects to leading remote or offshore teams effectively. At the outset of the relationship, every effort should be made to get face-to-face with the team in order to establish personal bonds. It doesn't matter if you visit them, or they visit you, or (ideally) both. These visits can be very special occasions, and with a few social outings combined, lifelong friendships can quickly develop. It's amazing how much more effective the working relationship becomes once people have met face-to-face.

Your communication style may need to be altered to take into account differing cultures. My own Australian culture can be quite direct and fast moving, which can seem confronting, even rude, to others. As a result, Aussies need to slow down and take a bit of a softer approach when dealing with people from other cultures (drinking less coffee helps). One of my biggest frustrations is when working with cultures where "yes" doesn't always mean yes. Sometimes it seems that "yes" can mean "I've heard you, I may or may not understand, and I have no idea if I really mean yes, but it seems like a good answer for the moment." I find this quite a challenge when partnered up with the Aussie approach. Patience, some indirect discussion circling around the topic, and some gentle questioning is usually effective in reaching a more precise understanding of the meaning of "yes." I've found that a good pattern to ensure that everything is clearly understood is to first discuss any plans etc., while writing it on a whiteboard. Then I'd wipe the whiteboard clean and have my offshore colleagues reproduce the plan again on the whiteboard. Then, for good measure, I'd send an email that night, confirming again what we'd agreed. With this approach, you'll need three strikes before you're out and "lost in translation."

Accents can also be an issue in communication, but usually only initially. People's ears soon tune in to the various distortions, and what at first seemed almost unintelligible quickly becomes understandable—something you won't even notice. It may seem as if they have the accent, but you have to remember—if someone else's accent sounds a bit strange to you, imagine how weird you sound to them!

Enjoy the cultural diversity, and welcome them into your teams and business life. They can only make your business stronger and more competitive.

Celebrations—Weddings, Parties, Any Reason at All!

In a similar vein to managing communications, it's a good idea to have a calendar of social events that range in scale from the big holiday bash to the Friday afternoon "sundowner" at the local bar. It's also best to vary the theme of the festivities, from casual family picnics to black-tie theater outings. This way, you can appeal to everyone's different tastes, which you'll ideally have in your diverse team. But be careful with participative sporting activities! Many people quickly find that the body isn't quite what it was when they were on the high school track team, and big swaths of your people probably have no interest whatsoever in banging into each other on the sporting field. The day after the event, work attendance can be noticeably impacted. But it does provide some entertainment in a pinch.

In recent years, there's been quite a shift in what's appropriate for work-related social events. The all-guy weekend fishing expeditions have mostly gone the way of the horse and buggy. Some organizations have a zero alcohol policy in place. In Japan some companies provide "I'm not drinking alcohol" buttons during company parties to give people an option to opt out. The once strong Australian culture of a "liquid lunch" has all but disappeared, and the litigiousness of American society has dampened enthusiasm for the Friday afternoon beer bash. Business lunches tend to be shorter, sharper, and more business than lunch. OK, it's not as much fun, but certainly more sensible.

Births, Deaths, and Marriages

The good, and the not so good, are an inevitable part of life. As the GM, you need to participate at an appropriate level in the major life events of your employees. Sending flowers and cards for celebrations and attending funerals to represent your company is really appreciated by your people and their families. It shows that you care about them as a person, which is the number three most motivating factor discussed in Bob Nelson's book, *1001 Ways to Reward Employees*. You also need to keep an eye out for anyone who is struggling so that help can be offered before it becomes a major problem and negatively impacts their work performance.

Someone suffering a long-term illness or major injury is another challenge that you are bound to encounter at some point in your career. Do whatever you can to keep this person's income flowing for as long as they are off work, either by discretionary pay or by arranging insurance. It will greatly reduce the stress on them and their family. I guarantee that you will be repaid double with loyalty and attitude once the person returns to work. This will also echo positively with the other members of the team. After all, it could be one of them next.

Recipe for Happy, Smiling People

You need to recruit the right employees with the right attitude into your organization. They need to be prepared, trained, and incentivized to enable the organization to meet the strategic goals. People bring their own level of intrinsic motivation, all you need to do is feed it—or at least avoid killing it off. That can largely be achieved via appropriate goal setting. Extrinsic motivation can be amplified via a sensible rewards system that is linked to the goals. The goals and rewards must encourage teamwork so that pooling of resources and knowledge spring naturally from the motivations of individuals on the team.

Your people will deeply appreciate being cared for as individuals and being given every opportunity for personal growth. At the end of the day, their success will contribute to your success. Invest in your people and they'll pay you the biggest returns of any area of your business.

chapter 7
Managing Relationships— External and Internal

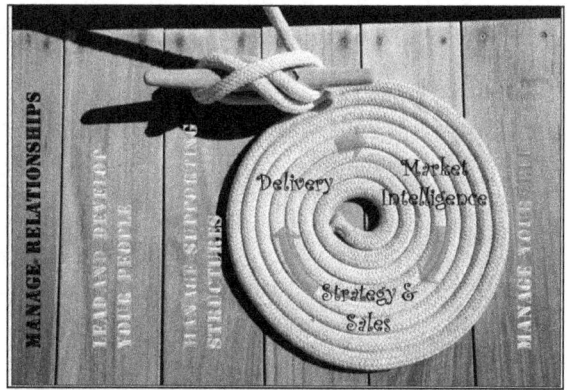

"It's much easier to build a relationship of trust with someone when you are sitting on the same side of the table."
– *Mitch Thrower, The Attention Deficit Workplace*

External Relationships—This Is Marketing as Well

As a Scrappy GM, you're in the people business (by now you should have noticed a repeating theme here). Maintaining external relationships is all part of the job. Those relationships will be with both your suppliers and with your customers. You'll want them to know that a strong relationship with you is good for them personally as well as their business. Creating good external relationships is an integral part of the ongoing marketing cycle. If you're going to win business repeatedly, it's only going to happen where you have solid customer relationships. Not the "the weather's been a bit hot lately" kind of relationships (the weather usually is hot in Australia, so there's no need to discuss it!), but a relationship where you know and understand the person you're dealing with personally and have built up a healthy level of trust with them.

Selling to buddies is a hell of a lot easier than selling to someone that you're barely acquainted to. This type of relationship does not come without effort. But, as there's no revenue to be made sitting around the office, you need to get your butt out there meeting people and building relationships that your competitors can't touch. Email, a poor substitute for true communication, can be done anytime, so use business hours for far more valuable face-to-face interactions.

SMALL BUSINESS TIP: Many small businesses involve short, sharp, one-off transactions with your customers. You can still get a relationship going with these people by striking up a conversation. Balinese people are natural masters at this. Their culture involves having a peaceful mind based on knowing where you've come from and where you are going. They like to check this with everyone they meet, therefore striking up an instant conversation. When you enter their shops, you're greeted with a huge smile, you tell them your life story, then you pay too much for something that you didn't want in the first place, and walk out with a grin on your face thinking, "How the hell did that happen?"

To establish and maintain an effective relationship you'll need to follow the same pattern of communication that you would with your own people (e.g., the "cone of communication" shown in Figure 10. Communicating in "the cone" means that you establish a pattern of interactions that range from the formal to the informal, adjusting the frequency as appropriate to make sure that you don't become a pain in the backside.

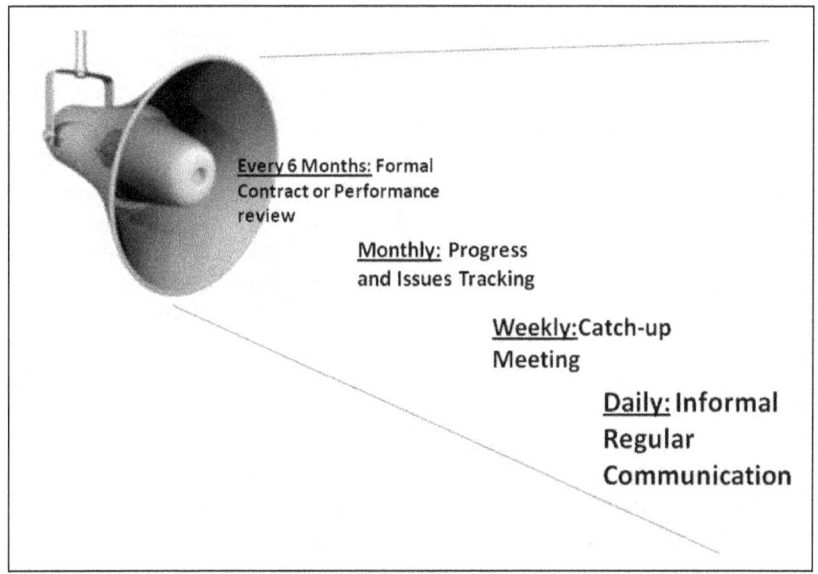

Figure 11: Cone of Communication for Customers

When meeting with people, even casually over coffee, be prepared! I always check in with my team to get the latest info and gossip on the person I'm meeting beforehand. Naturally, it's rather embarrassing to show up not knowing about some disastrous event that may have happened that morning, so a few minutes of preparation is well worth the effort. In my case, as an IT services provider, you want to make sure that there's no system problems before you start chatting up your client. Once I was late to a meeting with a bank in Kuala Lumpur due to a traffic jam, only to find out at the meeting that the jam had been caused by problems with our IT systems. Due to our system error, customers couldn't pay for their fuel purchases, and cars were queuing out onto the roads from petrol stations all along the shutdown. We'd gridlocked all of Kuala Lumpur, and I didn't even know about it. After learning that lesson the hard way, I always check in just before the meeting and have about six bullet points of the latest "events" to go over if need be. Keep in mind that you're there to see them, to be interested in them as individuals, and to care about their business. So listen to them! At least 70 percent of the talking should be done by them—and watch the body language. No gazing wistfully out the window, and, for heavens sake, don't you dare glance at your watch!

As far as meeting format, I think it's better to tailor it according to the person you're meeting. Some people feel more comfortable meeting in the office, others like to meet in a cafe. Dress according to your client's culture—a suit and tie for the government offices, but lose the tie in the mining environments. A good guideline is to dress just slightly better than the client. No matter what the culture is, wear your good gear. It's a sign of respect. Of course, there are the basic things, like always being on time. Early is annoying, late is shabby. If you are late, be sure to run the final few meters and appear to be out of breath (better yet, just be on time!).

Oh, and if it's a social occasion, all the same rules still apply—be prepared.

Who should you be meeting? That should be clear from the relationship maps that we covered in Chapter 3. Get to know these people's executive assistants, administrative assistants, and personal assistants. Don't underestimate the power of these low-status positions! They can move heaven and earth for you if you're on their good side—and make it hell if you're not. In fact, they carry so much organizational power that they should be on the relationship map as well!

Judging how your relationships are going is sometimes difficult, as client politeness and reluctance to disappoint can disguise serious issues. Relying on your own opinions and instincts is fraught with risk, as you can easily delude yourself that everything is rosy. It's too late to find out that you had a less than positive relationship when you lose or fail to gain a significant bit of business. Therefore, it's a great idea to involve a third party to check on how things are really going, someone with no skin in the game. The NPS surveys will give an indicator of how things are going, but a third-party interview will add richness and context to the numerical feedback. Not to be too philosophical, but if you feel reluctant to seek that feedback, that in itself is telling feedback.

SCRAPPY TIP: Look the part. When you show up for work, look like you're a GM. A great old mentor of mine many years ago said to me, "Always wear your very best clothes to work." He was a former U.S. Naval commander on the Hornet of Apollo 11, 12, and 13 fame, and he always looked very sharp in his dark suit, white shirt, and tie, and the shiniest shoes you've ever seen. His philosophy was that if you look the part, you'll get the part. It's all about improving the odds.

We Love Our Customers, but Some Are Really Difficult

Broadly speaking, there is no difference in dealing with difficult customers than the approach you would take when dealing with difficult staff. To some extent, the difference is that some customers, while difficult, are paying the bills, so you might give them a bit more leeway. You may think a person is a real asshole, but you are under no obligation to tell them that. If you have a personality clash with a critical client, alter your personality for the ten minutes that you need to deal with them—the same way that you'd adapt their culture.

However, just as a bad employee, the really bad apples of your customers are much better to cut loose, as their poor behavior will affect your staff, morale, and culture, and eventually start damaging your business. Illegal or unethical behavior is a no-brainer. Disengage from them. Even if you are a public service entity, your staff should not have to put up with bad or dangerous behavior, and steps need to be taken to protect them from it. We love airline stories, and there's the one about the Southwest Airlines executive who bought a verbally abusive customer a ticket on a competing airline—it built loyalty among the employees. (Legend has it that he said that both parties would be happier if the customer flew a different airline.)[27]

---

27. Lorraine Grubbs-West, *Lessons in Loyalty: How Southwest Airlines Does It—An Insider's View* (CornerStone Leadership Institute, 2005).

Entertainment that Doesn't Get You Sent to Hell

Entertainment is an important part of developing and maintaining external relationships, and it can take on many more forms than just a round of golf. People have many and varied interests, so organize events that appeal specifically to their tastes. We cover a wide range, from attending opera to getting behind the steering wheel of a racecar. Be careful! The aim here is to improve relationships through shared experiences not directly related to the business, not to bribe anyone, or set expectations of "I owe you one." And be respectful of cultural differences. You don't want to arrange a pig roast dinner for a delegation of vegetarians. And a group that includes women executives probably won't feel the same about "boys' night out" types of events as the boys do. While some women enjoy sports, not many will want to accompany you to a strip club. As surprising as it may be to some readers, this kind of activity is still a part of some business entertainment practices.

What the Heck Is Probity?

Most customers invoke a period of probity during their procurement cycle, where any participation in entertainment activities is temporarily suspended. You need to respect this ethical behavior, and look forward to celebrating together once the procurement activity is complete and you've won the business!

Internal Relationships—Getting the Best Possible Resources for Your Team (Without Ripping Someone Else Off!)

In larger organizations, internal relationships are vitally important in order for the Scrappy GM to be able to get the job done, and provide the team with every resource they need, whether it's "things," people, or money. There are numerous speed bumps in everyone's working lives, and you can breeze over some of them with the help of effective internal relationships, which will make your team a lot more productive. You'll be able to achieve success quicker and with less cost. This doesn't mean you'll make life more difficult for someone else, it means that you'll do what's sensible for the organization overall, working to find the win-win scenarios without all the fluff and bluster of egocentric political landscapes. Just like communicating with staff and customers, being effective internally means you need to get your "cone of communication" going—and the same rule of staying positive, positive, positive in anything written applies. Avoid incendiary emails like the plague. Definitely type them up (it will make you feel much better), but don't you dare hit the send button!

SCRAPPY TIP: Sometimes we are the problem. When it seems that everyone around you is acting like a horse's ass and you're not, perhaps have a think about it, as it may actually be that the opposite is true.

There is a key concept to keep in mind when you intend to create superior long-term internal relationships:

Don't Compete—Collaborate! And Don't Collaborate All by Yourself!

Competition might be good fun, but for you to win, somebody else has to lose, which is not a good idea if you all work in the same organization. Earlier in my career as a team leader, I used to love competing with other teams or departments, and had a whale of a time comparing my team's performance against theirs. Then one day we were sent to a leadership development course where we were presented with a challenge. This looked like great sport, so I immediately sought out a like-minded person, formed an alliance, and we quickly set about wreaking havoc on all the other team's efforts, while making sure that our own team achieved our goals. What I didn't realize was that the aim of the challenge was for all of the teams to be successful as a whole (as you would want in any organization). The other thing that I didn't realize was that the whole exercise was being recorded on video. My buddy and I finished our part of the challenge first, having scuttled everyone else's efforts, and we were very proud of ourselves. That is, until we were ushered into another room to watch the video replay of the afternoon's events. My newfound friend and I (both very sheepish at this point) were duly awarded a big fat FAIL for the day's leadership activities. Upon reflection, this experience really brought home to me how this very same attitude and approach had been impacting results back at work.

Make the pie bigger instead of arguing over who gets the bigger share of a tiny tart. In all areas of your organization, collaborate and encourage collaboration. Winning isn't about beating the other guy. It's about meshing with other parts of the organization, integrating your differences to create a stronger and more effective overall business machine. And while it is difficult, personal agendas (yours and theirs) need to be tempered, if not ignored. Your collaborative behavior will set an example for others.

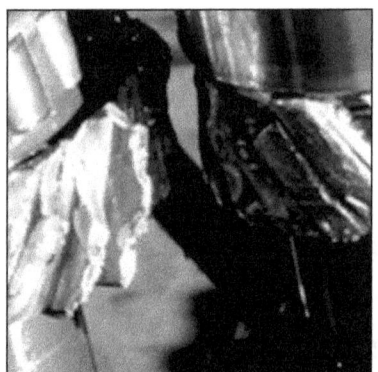

Figure 12: Competing Within the Organization Smashes the Gears—Collaborating Meshes It All Together!

SCRAPPY TIP: Social events are great opportunities to get to know your colleagues on another level, so make the effort to attend them and enjoy the interaction. But keep away from the BMW sessions (bitching, moaning, and whining), and stay upbeat. Whenever people fly in from other locations, they'll usually appreciate being taken out for dinner, and if they're from another country, they'll generally enjoy visiting your home for a meal. People are always curious to see how others live, particularly if they're from differing cultures, and opening up your home to them can make for a memorable occasion.

SCRAPPY TIP: Building relationships remotely is more of a challenge. If you happen to be remotely located compared to other parts of your organization, including your boss, they will only "see" very small slices of you and your work life. Therefore, make the most of any interactions. Make sure you always attend the phone and video conferences, joining the calls a few minutes early so that you can enjoy some informal banter. Covering the simple things, like having your action items and reports completed on time, will demonstrate reliability and put people at ease with your ability to run the remote part of the business. Some people don't cope well with the tyranny of distance, so anything you can do to lessen their anxiety will help minimize the "help" that flies in from head office.

Relationship Quality—Measuring the Unmeasurable

You'll want to periodically check on the status of your internal relationships and how effectively you're influencing those around you. This is not an easy thing to quantify, and we can all be blindsided at times as to our actual effectiveness in relationships. Counting how many people are willing to go out with you for beer and pizza after working hours is one rough indicator, but that's not going to check the relationship quality in a business sense. A more thorough method is to make use of something like the Human Synergistics-style tools, such as Leadership/Impact® assessment developed by Dr. Robert A. Cooke.[28] This is a form of 360-degree review that solicits feedback from your peers and from those who report directly to you. Normally a 360-degree review focuses on your performance and behavior. However, this review is the reverse in that it checks on how effectively you influence those around you to behave constructively and, therefore, is an effective method of measuring the quality of the relationships and your positive influence as a leader. The results will help you cut through the baloney, banter, and sucking up so that you can get an accurate picture of what's really going on.

Relationship Round-Out

Maintaining good external relationships is all part and parcel of the ongoing cycle of marketing. To excel in this area, making use of the "cone of communication," the same as you would with your people internally, will ensure a reliable set of interactions, without making a pain in the butt of yourself. While helpful, NPS surveys just aren't enough. There's no substitute for a meaningful personal relationship based on trust and mutual respect. Those kinds of relationships take time to build, so start early, well before you need to lean on the strength of those relationships, such as during a difficult business situation.

For great internal relationships, the approach is similar. Start with the "cone of communication," but with an additional focus on collaborating with your peers to achieve win-win scenarios. The competition is outside of your company, not within it. If you want to check on relationship quality in this area, some sort of 360-degree feedback is far more accurate than your offhand assessment of how you're doing. Get the data or risk being misled by your own skewed perspective.

Scrappy Quote: "You can't shake hands with a clenched fist." - *Gandhi*

---

28. Dr. Robert A. Cooke, *Leadership/Impact® (L/I)*, Plymouth MI: Human Synergistics International, 1997, http://www.humansynergistics.com.

chapter 8
Managing Yourself

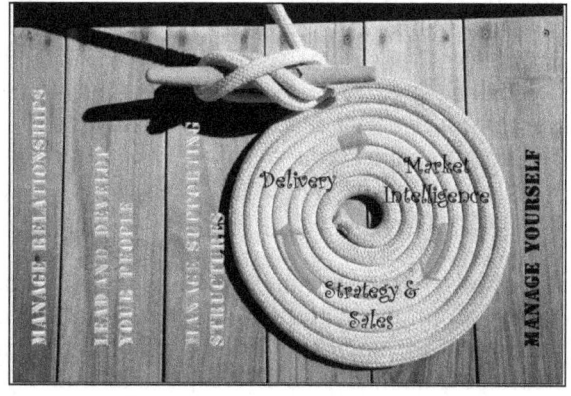

"Lead yourself, lead your superiors, lead your peers, and free your people to do the same. All else is trivia."
– *Dee Hock, Founder of VISA International.*

In the previous chapters of this book, we have concentrated on things other than yourself: setting strategy for your organization, marketing, selling, running the business, and managing relationships. They're all activities external to yourself. This chapter is all about *you*. The reason being, if you are effectively managing yourself, physically and mentally, then it's going to be a lot easier to be effective in managing the business. And if you're having a hoot at the same time, it will be icing on the cake!

You Are Being Watched

Everyone watches their boss. The feeling of being watched was something that I was initially a bit uncomfortable with. People's interest was to be expected, as my appointment to the GM role was a surprise to many of my co-workers. So there were definitely people sizing me up—judging my capability to actually do the job. Just walking around the building had people's heads popping up above the workstations like a family of meerkats. As time passed and things progressed, my confidence grew, and I got used to "The Watchers," accepting their behavior as normal curiosity. I won't say that I enjoy it. (Some people do seem to get off on it, and if that's your cup of tea, then good luck to you. Just don't go overboard basking in the glory. No one likes a self-absorbed blowhard.)

So what's this "Watcher" phenomenon all about? In Chapter 7 we spoke about obtaining feedback via some sort of 360-degree review, such as the Human Synergistics tool,[29] and how your actions and activities influence others. Well, this is where you apply what you've learned about yourself. There's plenty of evidence that emotions are contagious.[30] If you are the GM, and you're stressed, your people will reflect that stress. If you're not taking things too seriously, neither will your team. If you're able to take a constructive approach, your team will mirror that approach, and you'll be able to tackle problems with a constructive frame of mind. I've been lucky enough to be able to track feedback on my performance over a period of almost ten years and compare it to feedback of the teams that I was managing at the various

---

29. Dr. Robert A. Cooke, *Leadership/Impact® (L/I)*, Plymouth MI: Human Synergistics International, 1997, http://www.humansynergistics.com.
30. Christine Nyholm, "Happiness Is Contagious in Harvard Study," *Suite101.com*, December 22, 2008, http://bit.ly/contagious_happiness social-therapy.suite101.com/article.cfm/happiness_is_contagious_in_harvard_study.

points in that period. It was somewhat freaky how close the team's performance mirrored feedback on my own. As my performance profile improved, so did the team's.

So, what? Well, at the same time as the team's profile improved towards more constructive behaviors, so did the financial indicators and results. That should have every GM dancing in the cafeteria. To add icing to the cake, customer satisfaction and references to other potential clients also had a marked improvement. Coincidence? I don't think so.

Below is a sample of the results, with the feedback being given via the Human Synergistics tool.[31] This tool is a feedback mechanism, along the lines a 360-degree review, where people that work with you—peers, subordinates and bosses—fill out a multiple-choice questionnaire on either individual (yours) or group behaviors. The results are charted showing biases in behavior styles in three major groupings: constructive styles, aggressive/defensive styles and passive/defensive styles. Research has shown that success in all measures is more readily achieved by people who take a constructive approach to their work (and life). This is something that I've experienced to be true myself. Below, the first two charts (Figure 13) show my profile in 1999 and that of the group that I was managing at the time. At that time, my Leadership/Impact® report showed a great deal of approval behaviors with a sprinkling of constructive behaviors. (Nothing but upside staring me in the face back then!) As a result, the team's Organizational Culture Inventory® profile is oppositional and competitive, with little in the way of constructive behaviors. (Of course I blamed it on them—more of my avoidance behaviors manifesting themselves).

The next two charts (Figure 14) show my profile in 2007, after several reviews. By then I'd worked out how much impact my behaviors had on the team's behaviors. The last radar diagram shows the team's profile in 2007. In this case the team's profile is significantly more constructive and I can vouch that the flow on affect to the business results, in regards to revenue growth and profitability, has been remarkable.

---

31. Dr. Robert A. Cooke, *Leadership/Impact® (L/I)*, Plymouth MI: Human Synergistics International, 1997, http://www.humansynergistics.com.

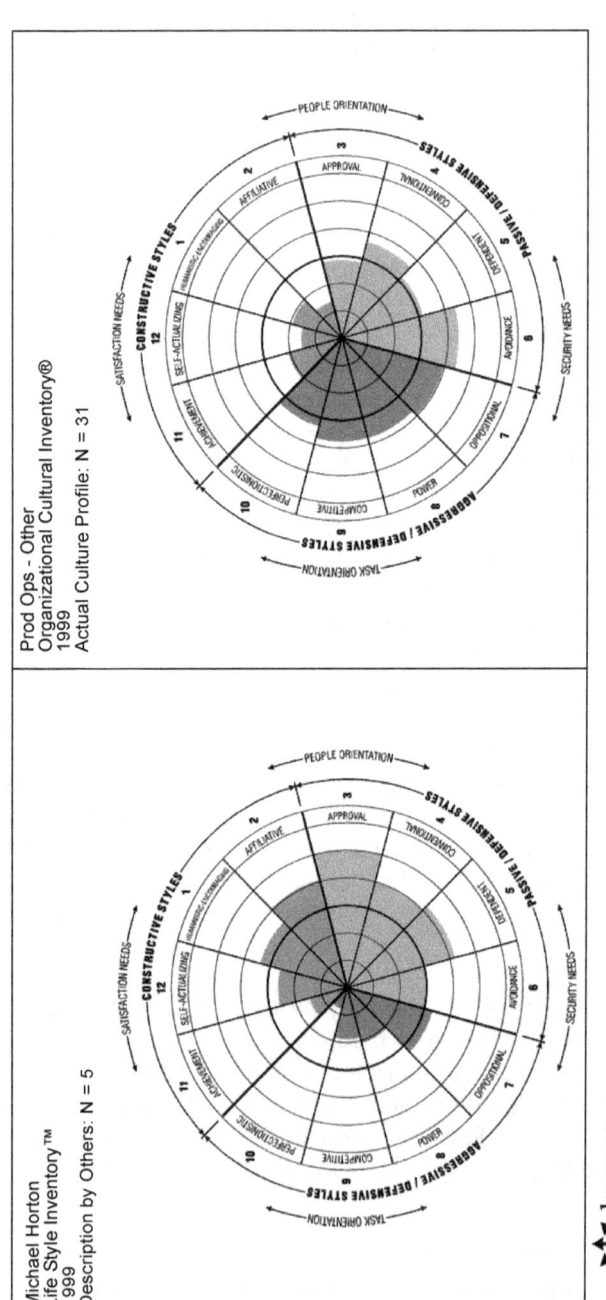

Figure 13: My Profile (left), an Approval and Dependence Style, and the Team's Profile (right) in 1999.

For a pdf copy of these images, please go to: http://happyabout.com/scrappyabout/humansynergistics-images.pdf

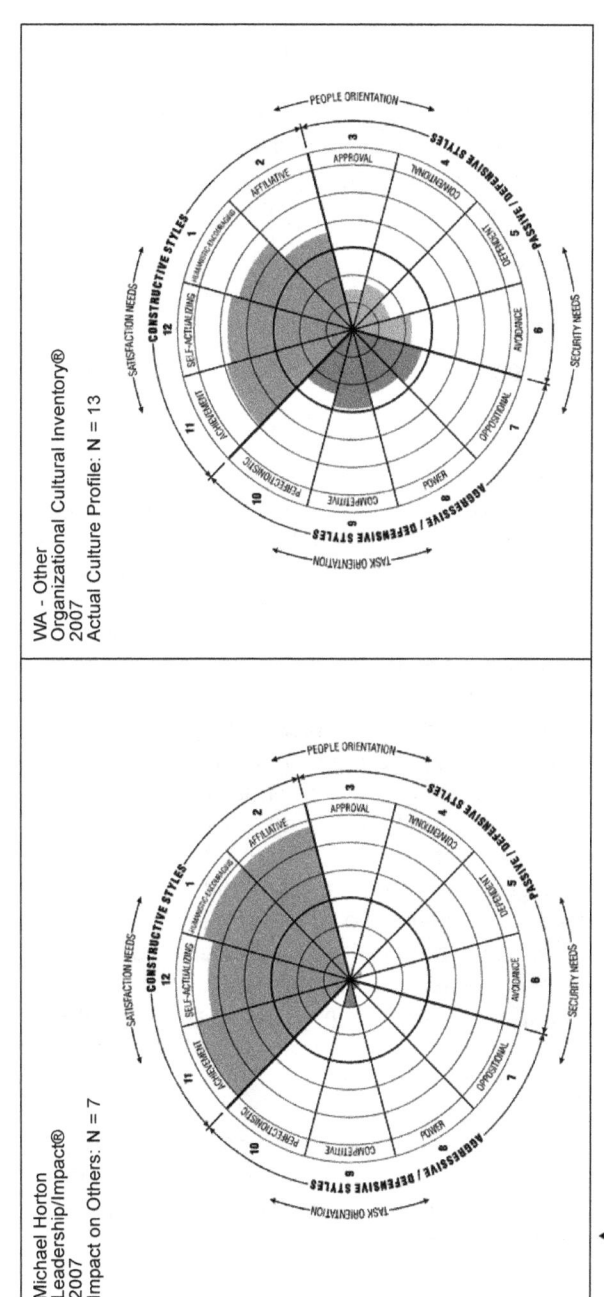

Figure 14: By 2007, My Style (left) Has Become More Constructive, as Has the Team's (right). The Change was Correlated With Greatly Improved Business Performance.

For a pdf copy of these images, please go to: http://happyabout.com/scrappyabout/humansynergistics-images.pdf

SCRAPPY TIP: There's a well-known saying that "people leave managers, not companies."[32] It may be that there is just a personality or cultural mismatch, but, in general, I subscribe to this idea: if your people respect your leadership and you can evoke some personal loyalty, it will go a long way towards keeping people from leaving your company and keeping the team intact and stable.

Your Management Style—It's All about Leadership

Just as we all have different personalities and profiles, we also have differing management styles. Those styles will range from autocratic (probably not so effective over the long term with people whose success depends on them thinking for themselves) to coaching (likely to be more effective, especially with highly intelligent, creative, self-motivated professionals). You can use any of the plethora of feedback mechanisms available to explore and understand your management style. These tools are useful ways to get to know yourself, so that you can understand and work on your blind spots and weak points, and capitalize on your strong points. Just like most human beings, I never really understood myself, or what I did as a manager, or why it worked. I knew that what I was doing worked, but because I didn't understand why, I was hard pressed to be able to repeat my successes. This all changed when I attended a weeklong management course that concentrated on helping me to understand my behaviors. A psychologist explained these behaviors, and their affect on others, to me at the end of the week. It was relatively painless. I didn't have to lie on a couch or talk about my childhood. Anyhow, I learned quite a bit about my mother's favorite person—me. I'd always thought that I was reasonably introverted, maybe even shy. To my surprise, I found that, in reality, I was an extrovert who was hiding my abilities—a strange combination. But when I dug a bit deeper, I realized that it actually meant I was being lazy—not letting people know what I could do—so that I could take things easy and just cruise along. This was a great

---

32. Marcus Buckingham and Curt Coffman, *First, Break All the Rules: What the World's Greatest Managers Do Differently (Simon & Schuster, 1999)*, page number.

revelation to me, and made me think, "Hey! I've got to get off my backside, communicate and share thoughts and knowledge with the other peeps working here!" (Interestingly, when discussing this afterwards with my wife, she said, "You bloody idiot, I could have told you that!" Oh.) Bottom line, you've got to know yourself to be effective in leading others. There are thousands of ways to do this. Pick one and get busy! Listening to your spouse is just one possibility.

Understanding myself better has improved my business leadership effectiveness greatly. I'm more able to predict reactions that I'll get from others, influence people positively, and, therefore, more able to create predictable and repeatable successes. Jump at any opportunity to do get to know yourself better! Whenever opportunity knocks, accept the "gift" of some feedback on your style from someone close to you whose opinion you respect. It may include some messages that you don't want to hear, but listen and learn. Just like receiving any gift, always say "thank you" even if you don't like it all that much.

One More Time—Collaborate, Don't Compete!

We've covered this one in Chapter 6 under internal relationships, but I'll emphasize it again as it was one of my big failures in the past. Competition with your peers is a short-term strategy, and shortsighted as well. Collaboration is the long-term winning strategy—enhancing your organizational network and creating goodwill that can be drawn on when you need it. Favors done today to help your peers may be paid back in double at a later date. And, similar to assisting sales efforts via strategic alliances—where the use of partnering can be done to eliminate strong competitors and strengthen your own sales efforts—collaborating with your peers strengthens your internal influence.

SCRAPPY TIP: Look out for others. You haven't reached your position in the organization solely by your own efforts. A few years back a very wise man advised me that those of us who are more capable have a sacred duty to look after those who are less capable. What's more, it's in your selfish best interest. Helping others is one of the most practical ways to help yourself in business. Usually the people we're helping are customers, but we also need to think about our "internal" customers and help them, too.

Help Your Boss Meet Their Targets

Everyone has a boss, and every boss has a set of targets. Want to be wildly popular with your boss? Get to know what their targets are, how they fit into the overall business strategy, and how you can contribute to meeting them. There's no rocket science here—help your boss make their targets and you will fulfil the personal "what's in it for me" (WIIFM). Consequently, they'll be a lot more interested in you. This isn't sucking up to the boss. It's a pragmatic approach for ensuring your success in your organization. A business-case pitch will be a much easier sell when it directly references how it will contribute to making your boss successful. As a part of the natural order of things, your "usefulness" to your boss will ensure that you will be looked after and rewarded as a matter of course... and you'll most likely never have to ask for a pay rise again (unless your boss is a bombastic buffoon who mistakenly believes that he's single-handedly responsible for his success).

Similarly, make sure that those who report to you know your goals and targets so that they can contribute to achieving them. All this "contributing" will go a long way towards making the world a happier place—well, at least YOUR world!

Balance—No Such Thing, but Give It a Shot!

"Few people do business well who do nothing else."
– Philip Stanhope, 4th Earl of Chesterfield (1694-1773)

Achieving a balanced lifestyle is one of the most important factors to long-term success, a healthy life, and avoiding being a boring old fart. To fulfill your obligations as a Scrappy GM, you need to be able to show up to work with a smile on your face—every day, day in, day out—for as long as you bear the responsibility of that role. Life is a numbers game, a game of chance. What's the probability of you getting ill, injured, suffering cancer, or mental illness? Who knows! But, what you can do is improve your odds. To do this, you'll need to create and maintain balance in your life, whatever the heck that is.

Balance is an individual thing. What is normal to others in regards to how they create balance in workload, family, leisure, etc., is not necessarily normal for you, so don't go trying to model yourself on someone else. Some people think that working sixty or seventy hours a week is normal, even effortless, and they even enjoy it! That doesn't mean that you have to put in those kinds of hours. Your balanced "normal" can be completely different. Me, I can tell when I'm in balance by whether or not I get a headache. When my balance goes kaflooy—too much work, too much stress, or, even the other way, too much play and not enough sleep—I'll get a migraine headache. Migraines eschew routine, so when my life's routine gets out of wack, my head tells me. For better or for worse, I have a built-in personal balance monitor. If you haven't already worked out what your personal balance monitor is, have a look around. It will be there somewhere, your weight goes up or down, a rash breaks out, your wife leaves you, partner moves out, your pet dog won't look at you, clerks at the grocery roll their eyes when they think you're not looking, other drivers flip you the bird—something along those lines.

So, what's the meaning of balance? It's the appropriate distribution of your time and effort across what's important in your life. The experts on this say that your life is ideally divided into four dimensions: work, family, community, and self. Everyone has a different perspective, so interpret this as is fitting for you. For me, balance means getting home each night for dinner, not travelling more than 30% of the time, getting involved with schools and universities to help out where I can, and staying involved in my favorite activities, surfing and sailing. The key is that you need to think about more than just work. So, let phone calls go to voice mail and email pile up to high heaven, and get out there and enjoy yourself now and then!

Looking after your health is an obvious priority for people concerned with peak performance. Obviously, you don't want to be packing an extra couple dozen pounds, kilograms, or whatever unit of measure you happen to use to track your largesse. Your brain is part of your body, too, so if your body is working sluggishly, so will your brain. You can't expect to run a business effectively for any length of time if you're not reasonably healthy. So part of that balance is to maintain your health and fitness level. Do yoga. Jog. Dance. Plant a garden. Just don't be a slug!

Ongoing education of yourself is also important—adding dimensions to yourself that compliment what's already there. Become a lifelong learner. It doesn't matter if it's a formal course or self-study, whatever's your cup of tea, just keep learning! New knowledge opens new doors, and sometimes a window or a smokestack, in what we do and how we think. It keeps us interested and keeps the energy levels up. None of us will ever know everything in our particular fields—the more you get to know, the more you realize how much more there is to know. Learning keeps you humble!

Worry and stress—don't! It's wasted energy. Plan for the future, but don't worry about it. Live and work in the present moment. Keep one eye on the horizon, but both hands on the wheel. Come to grips with your limits as well as your capabilities. You gotta eat. You gotta sleep. You gotta take time to relax and refresh. If you can achieve a reasonably balanced life as you define it, the stress (and the headaches) will look after themselves.

Who's Really Running the Joint?

You're going to need to need some good, supportive help—a good executive assistant (EA), for example. (Find one who's read the entertaining book *Sitting on a File Cabinet, Naked, With a Gun: True Stories of CEO Assistants in Silicon Valley*.[33] Chances are they're a cut above the rest!) EAs and AAs (administrative assistants) are the secret society that exists within organizations—the informal power brokers. In a very real sense, they run many companies. The only reason they don't have the corner office is that many of them have a few impediments to holding the official title of GM: they are women (a very small percentage of GMs are women), or they didn't finish their college education. But don't be stupid! These people are incredibly capable and influential. Change management gurus say that if you want to implement change more easily, seek out the opinion leaders. These people easily fit that description. Everyone talks to them, they're very supportive of each other, and they act as the informal ethics and morality committee in many organizations. And they have the ear of the top executives. Even Miss Money Penny has James Bond under control!

If you are lucky enough to have an AA or EA, choose one who is a master of influence. This role requires tact, finesse, and an enormous amount of emotional intelligence. Your choice of who fills that role will be key to your success and that of your businesses. This person is the front window to your organization, and your business's competence, will be judged at this first touch point. Choose someone who will work to support you—definitely not someone who will compete with you or undermine you. This needs to be a close partnership that cannot be subject to divide and conquer techniques that will inevitably be deployed by people trying to get their way. It is almost a marriage; but on that point, ensure, at all costs, that there is a very clear line between work life and home life (you know what I mean). Any crossing of the line is going to upset the natural balance of things, and disaster is bound to follow! Froggy should definitely NOT go courting!

---

33. Linda McFarland and Joan Linden, *Sitting on a File Cabinet, Naked, With a Gun: True Stories of Silicon Valley CEO Assistants* (AuthorHouse, 2009).

A Few More Basics of the GM Life—Presentation and Media Skills

You're standing in front of three hundred people, and they're all looking expectantly at you, waiting to hear words of inspiration and wisdom, to hear you impart all that knowledge that is reputably rattling around in that Scrappy GM head of yours. Oops! Your mind has gone completely blank, and all of that knowledge, expertise, and people skills have temporarily vanished from your memory banks due to the stress of standing up in front of all of these nice folks. There's nothing—just blankness, a dry mouth, and a croaky throat. But you shuffle your notes, adjust the microphone, take a sip of water, and stumble forward. "Let's get started," you chirp in your best adolescent nasal squeal. "Oh, joy," thinks the audience. But pretty soon the adrenalin kicks in, the brain gets whirring, and, before you know it, you're into a reasonably coherent flow.

Presentation skills are an age-old chestnut for most people. If you want to get anyone unfamiliar with presenting out of their comfort zone, stick them in front of a few hundred people and then check their pulse rate. I was worse than awful when I started in the GM game. For me, this was the most terrifying part of stepping into the GM role. People smiled politely as they listened to my mumbling and stumbling, and the company invested plenty of money in my presentation skills, which gradually made a big positive difference. Whatever the cost in time and effort, this is one of the best investments you will make as a leader. If you want to be able to lead large groups of people, you have to be able to communicate with them. Presentations are a big part of that. I took on the challenge like a kid eating an ice cream cone on a hot summer day.

Act 1. Scene 1. Take 1. An actor was brought in to give me some pointers—and he stuck me in front of a camera straight away. He then insisted that I do twenty presentations on the hop, with the topics thrown at me at random and zero preparation. That was the easy part! The really painful part was that I then had to sit there and watch each presentation. Ugh! I'd rather have been drawn and quartered by razorback hogs! It took all morning and gave me blisters on my throat, but ultimately it was worth it. My confidence increased, and soon I could feel myself taking my focus off of my inner dialogue and directing it onto my audience, where every speaker's attention belongs. This shift in focus did away with my nervousness.

I experienced more speaking remedies than Carter has pills, but the three things that really helped were:

1. Practice—seize every opportunity (the first five hundred times are the hardest).
2. Speak from the heart and in your own natural style (people spot fakes).
3. Forget about yourself and concentrate on your audience.

Dealing with the media, particularly in written form, is something I find much easier. If you follow the Golden Rule we've already discussed of positive, positive, positive—and don't breach any confidences—you won't go wrong there. Many organizations have special public relations people for covering media releases. They're pros! Work with them, follow their advice, and you'll always have a great result.

The Lowdown on Looking after Yourself

- Accept that you will be under scrutiny, so walk the talk. There's nothing worse than a GM who says one thing and does another.
- Understand yourself, your management style, where you need to improve, and how you can play to your strengths. Then play to them!
- Design and live a balanced life that provides time for yourself: health, personal growth, work, family, and some other hobby or interest.
- Get good help around the office. Your choice of EA can make or break you!
- Become an extraordinarily effective communicator—in real life and in written form.
- Enjoy yourself! Or at least look like it. Remember, you're being watched.

Oh, yeah—and don't compete, collaborate! No one gets to the top without a few shoves from below.

SCRAPPY TIP: Regarding office layout, pay attention to how your desk is positioned to make your office welcoming rather than officious. You don't want it to look like a great big command post. Make it cheerful and inviting. Have a cozy conversation nook with a small table and a couple of chairs for informal chats that deemphasizes the power differential between you and others (let's be real here —everyone knows you are the GM, but when you are sitting in the same damn uncomfortable chair they are, well, it's a start). And clean out the crap regularly. (I set a goal of throwing out at least three handfuls of "stale" paperwork per week.) If you haven't touched it in a month, it's probably not going to be touched again (and probably didn't need to be printed in the first place, now that you mention it). Oh, and sometimes cleaning up the office symbolically helps you clean out your mind. Scrappy bonus!

chapter

9 Salute to Supporting Services, Processes, and Structures

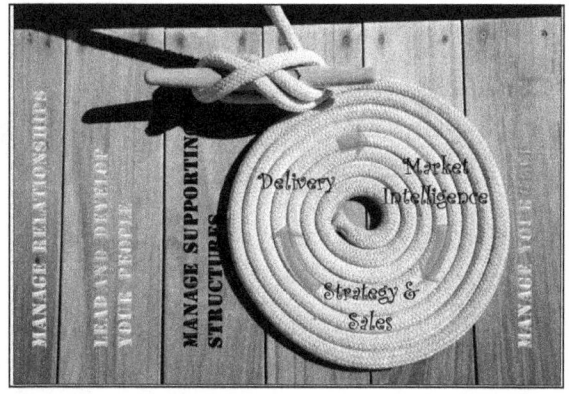

"Business is not just doing deals; business is having great products, doing great engineering, and providing tremendous service to customers. Finally, business is a cobweb of human relationships."
– H. Ross Perot, American Businessman

In successfully running your business, you'll need to navigate a maze of processes and interactions with entities both within your organization and with third parties. The value-add that they provide is critical to your successful operation. One strand of silk doesn't make a cobweb. You're going to need lots of strands to catch your daily meal. (See Figure 15.) Get good at fostering mutually beneficial relationships among all stakeholders if you want to run and grow a successful business for the long term.

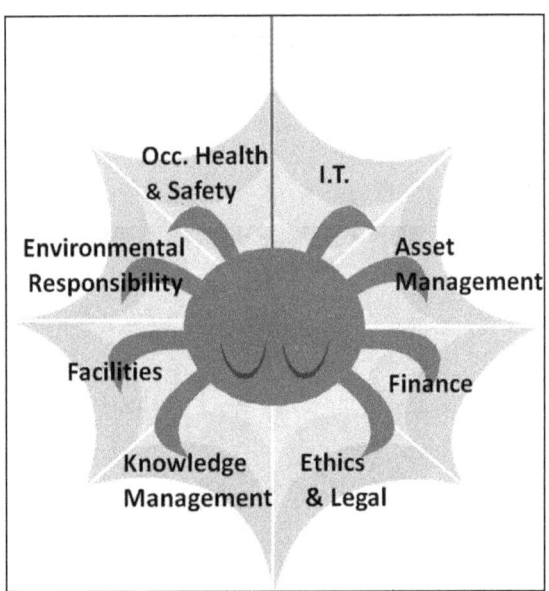

Figure 15: Your Web of Supporting Services

This chapter is all about avoiding those calamities and catastrophes that have given this book its subtitle. The people we're saluting here are those in the support roles that will assist you in running your business effectively, and in the worst case, keep you out of jail! Then there's the infrastructure and technology available to ensure that your business is competitive. Depending on the size of your business and your preferences, the services can be provided in-house or by a third party. On that decision, I don't think there's any right or wrong answer. Whatever floats your boat. The key is that you view these services as key to your success, use them to your advantage, and don't view them as merely a necessary evil. You can travel in a car without a proper suspension/support system, but it's a rough ride.

Googles and Gadgets

Having been in the IT services industry for eons, this feels like home turf for me. And if anything can encapsulate what I've learned over the decades in this industry, it is KEEP IT SIMPLE AND SENSIBLE. Wherever possible with software solutions, go vanilla and straight-out-of-the-box. This is one place where thinking outside of the box can get you into big trouble.

If out-of-the-box doesn't fit your processes, consider changing your process to fit! It could end up a much cheaper and easier approach. My view is that any customization is akin to introducing a genetic disorder into your IT. It might be benign, but there's a good chance that it will attack your capital budget like a ferocious cancer when first implemented, and reappear to attack your future budgets many times over—in fact, every time that a hardware or software vendor introduces a new generation of operating system, database, or application. Keeping it simple, and avoiding customization, will reduce your costs—and that wide-eyed fear of the unstoppable "progress" in technology in the rest of your organization.

The other great thing about un-customized systems is that you are more readily able to take advantage of "cloud-computing offerings" to satisfy your business's IT requirements.[34] If you're able to take advantage of cloud-style infrastructure and services, you'll remove a good many of the headaches and costs that IT systems force upon you.

There may be times when you'll need to integrate multiple applications in order to accommodate an end-to-end data flow. Seek the help of experienced professionals to do this, as again it will remove a good chunk of the headaches and put a lid on the costs.

Need an IT Technologist? Hell No! Just Ask a Teenager!

Seriously, teenagers are fantastic e-communicators, and they love doing things on the cheap, even free whenever possible. (Watch out though, as teenagers' moral and ethical compasses are still very much under construction.) They seem to have an innate ability to exploit the hell out of whatever resources are available to them, cheaply and easily. So, what better place to start than to check out what they're "into" at present. And, if it's something new—and it will be, as it's their habit to be different from the generation before them-have a think about how this can be utilized in your business. A great example is social networking: Twitter, Facebook, YouTube, and the like. Originally scoffed at by "serious" business people and taken to with great enthusiasm by the teenage population, social media now forms a credible base for business communication and knowledge sharing, as well as being an incredibly powerful medium for marketing-so-called "social media marketing," or SMM for short. The teenage population, while lacking the prestige of *Harvard Business Review*, is a source of valuable leading indicators for business trends. Whatever teenagers are into now, you can be sure that it will become mainstream within a few years.

---

34. Eric J. Brown and William A. Yarberry, *The Effective CIO: How to Achieve Outstanding Success through Strategic Alignment, Financial Management, and IT Governance* (Auerbach Publications, 2009), Chapter 13.

Security and Backups

In these days of hackers, identity theft, and computer viruses, the security of your IT systems needs to be taken extremely seriously—there is no margin for error here. And what appears secure today can end up being totally insecure overnight after someone releases their latest havoc—inducing code onto the Internet. Anyone who's suffered a major virus attack knows how crippling and frustrating this experience can be. I, for one, leave this area totally to the pros. If you have in-house security people, great—just make sure that they're absolutely keeping things up to date. Otherwise get contract help or, as a last resort, study up yourself (e.g., *Scrappy Information Security: The Easy Way to Keep the Cyber Wolves at Bay* by Michael Seese). Cloud computing adds a whole new dimension in the security area, so you may find yourself having a two-tier approach to your security policies—one set of policies around the information held on the traditional in-house systems and another for data that's free to move into the cloud-based systems.

Backups: yeah, yeah, yeah, everyone says that they are doing them, but are you really? Have you tried recovering your data? It's amazing how many people find that the data that they've been dutifully backing up for years cannot be successfully restored in the event a need arises. And just because you can restore it doesn't mean you can access it. As platforms change, can the data that you're required to keep for years for statutory requirements be read today? Do you even backup your own laptop or handheld? These are questions that you (or your responsible people) must truthfully answer. Everyone's busy. There are always "reasons," but that won't save you when disaster strikes. Have I seen the worst happen? Absolutely—numerous times—and I've also seen the resultant tears. Real ones. Don't let it happen!

Jettison the Computer Room—It's Astronomically Expensive!

Talk about simple! Outsource it, or take advantage of cloud computing. But if, for some reason, you simply must have your very own computer room, the following things need to be considered:

- Location: Choose one that is flood, earthquake, fire, and bomb risk-free.
- Security: Can some drunken idiot drive a vintage troop carrier through the wall? Yep, this actually happened. I've seen the tragic results.
- Air-conditioning: Servers are getting ever smaller, so we can cram even more into the computer room—but there's a lot of hot air in there.
- Floor structures: I've seen second-story concrete slabs drop three inches due to heavy weight of high-density disk arrays and years of cables stacked on top of each other.
- Power conditioning: There never seems to be enough capacity, and someone's always complaining about the noise from emergency power generators. Years ago we had a guy arrive at work while one such generator was running. It was so loud in the underground carpark that he got out of his car and accidently left the engine running. At 3 p.m. that afternoon, there was a terrible screeching noise from the car followed by a building full of smoke.
- Cabling: It's expensive, gets left under the floor, builds up over the years, and next thing the architects are complaining that the concrete floor has a big banana bend in it (see "floor structures" above).
- Monitoring: The only thing that seems to be getting easier.

As I've said, it's all too hard and too expensive. If you can sensibly get rid of your computer room and make it somebody else's headache, jump in and take full advantage of the opportunity.

Keeping Track of Your IT Assets

Naturally, in large organizations with lots of people there will also be large fleets of IT assets. IT asset management is the black art of all black arts. I spent several years attempting to manage large fleets of IT assets, and it was damn near impossible to get asset tracking accuracy above 90 percent. And that's just looking at the hardware.

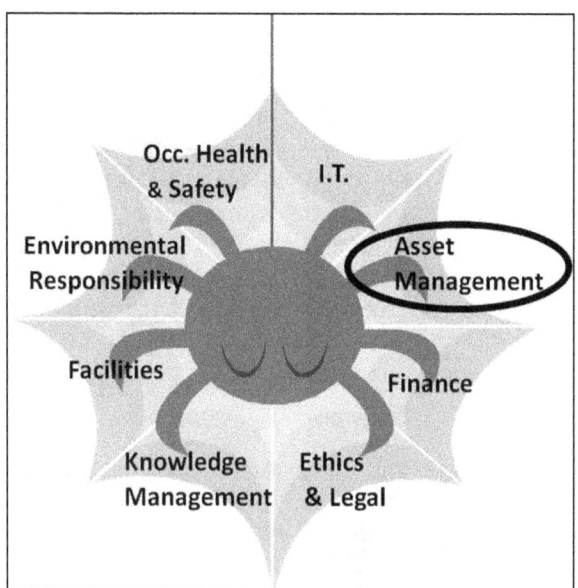

(Sure, I hear you scoff and say to yourself, "It's certainly not that bad here." Well, do a test for yourself. Ask for a copy of the asset register, walk out of your office, and see how many matches you get with any IT assets that are within twenty paces—be prepared for a shock!)

The need to track software just compounds the problem. If you have a fleet of ten thousand desktops and laptops, each one of those assets is going to have upwards of one hundred and fifty different pieces of software residing on it, so suddenly you have 1.5 million items to try and keep track of—and then you're likely to be trying to track four fields of data for each of those, usually the serial number, model, owner, and cost center or location. So, in theory, you could be attempting to track six million pieces of data (of course much of this can be automated). Add to that the fact that people are constantly moving gear around, loading new software, swapping bits and pieces, and taking gear home. Individuals tend to think, "It's only one little printer; it won't matter if I take it with me when I move to my new department." The thing is, EVERYONE IS THINKING THE SAME THING. This is one of the major cost areas in any organization, and it is always one big "Holy Toledo!" situation when someone tries to tick and tie the asset inventory.

What's a simple and sensible strategy for this situation? I think there are two extremes. On the perfectionist side of things, you could have software-based monitoring tools scanning the network, coupled with opportunistic checking when there is a physical "touch" of the asset, triangulated with an asset number check every time someone calls the help desk. With some hard work over a period of six months or more, you can get the asset accuracy percentage up above 90 percent. If you really want to nail the asset register, the use of RFID technology is becoming viable, with automated scanning as equipment is moved around.

I think a more simple and practical approach is to structure your procurement practices and financing around not having to track the assets throughout their useful life. For hardware, expense the purchases, rather than capitalizing them—and trap the "sensibleness" of the purchase at the time of purchase with a clear message of "don't come back and ask for another one if you lose it." One colleague who worked at HP told me that all small ticket items such as computers and printers are simply expensed in order to avoid the onerous task (and expense!) of tracking them. For software (right to use, as you can rarely "own" software), set up enterprise-style agreements with your software vendors that have "true ups" in arrears. This way either only one software scan a year is required, and you can look forward to paying only what's fair usage, not single-point payments on multiple versions of software that inevitably get left dormant on systems. At many large companies a "Common Operating Environment" is established on every IT-supported PC, and is verified upon each connection to the internal network. Updates are pushed out automatically from a central server, and can be tracked there as well.

SCRAPPY TIP: Pesky Leases—Where the hell are all those laptops I'm paying leases for? Leases are a great way of keeping assets off the balance sheet and can be a cost effective way of managing your IT hardware requirements (or any asset for that matter). BUT, watch out! There's massive upside for the underwriter (the entity providing the cash) if you don't (or can't) return the asset at the end of the primary lease period. Check those end-of-lease return clauses in the contract, as many will have you locked into automatic renewals for failure to return on time and in good condition. Some contracts basically lock you into a "pay this lease forever" loop if you lose or damage the leased goods. This loop can be very expensive to break out of. (Agilent has actually started leasing all of their PCs and trading them in every three years. If your computer is stolen, you need to produce a police report to get a replacement. If it's just lost, heaven help you—it's better that you were mugged in an alley so at least you'd have the police report!)

A Desk for Everyone and Everyone's Desk in the Budget

There's a good quote that describes the difference between managers and leaders: "Managers trust numbers; leaders trust people, who then understand and use numbers."[35] People often ask, "How do you manage the finances so easily?" Well, I think it's simple, black and white: there's either enough money or there's not. You're either making enough revenue and profit, or you're not.

---

35. Pat Townsend and Joan Gebhart, "What Happened to Quality?" *Quality Digest*, 1998, http://www.qualitydigest.com/feb98/html/townsnd.html.

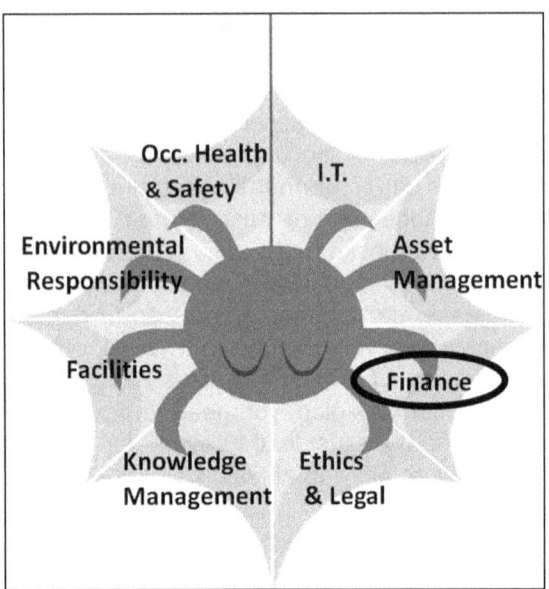

The key to running a profitable business is to take in at least a penny more than you shell out. You don't have to be a financial wizard, but you do need to know which questions to ask and when to raise them. If there is something confusing, then quiz your finance people until they give you an answer that you can understand. My experience is that if it's difficult to make heads or tails of the current financial situation, then something's cooking... and it's not likely to be pumpkin scones. Accruals, deferrals, balance sheet holdings, and book values are all handy cooking ingredients, so turn the heat up on them if they do not smell sweet.

Reports from the finance system need to be clear and consistent—consistent, so that the management team becomes familiar and relaxed about reading and interpreting the reports. This way the energy can be focused on making decisions based on the financial feedback, rather than looking dazed at the report (and not owning up that they don't understand it).

Never agree to a suicide budget. If you do, the likely outcome is that both you and your boss will end up looking stupid... three times: the first time is midway through the year when you fess up to not running on track; then again when you accept the challenge to get back to budget; then a third time when you don't make budget at the end of the year. And depending on how things sit, it may be the last time! Conversely, never agree to a cushy budget. You'll be a labeled a "sandbagger" (sand bags are emptied towards the end of the year to lighten the boat). Overachieving too much will only get your peers offside, and they'll be out to torpedo your light boat at the next possible chance.

As you can see, the ideal budget is a balancing act—and as a rule of thumb your good budgeting would have you keeping within plus or minus 2 or 3 percent of your targets and demonstrating an in-control and well-run business. This is whether it is revenue, cost, or both. While extra revenue is always welcomed, it is even more welcomed when it is forecast. If things have gone really well during the year, then re-forecast. And if they've not gone so well, re-forecast. DO NOT hide bad news, as stories on "bad books" leak like a sieve. Everyone loves to share a horror story, especially if it's about someone else's misfortunes.

Let's be clear here—financials are not a goal, they are a tool to improve decision making. In advance of a decision, they provide insights to improve the quality of the decision. After the fact, they provide feedback on the quality of that decision. Revenue, growth, and profit are not targets, they are feedback that your business decisions have been effective. GMs that fall into the trap of having strictly financial targets miss the whole point of financial analysis, and certainly don't qualify to be called Scrappy... well, maybe if we drop the "S."

SCRAPPY TIP: Every organization uses a soup of acronyms and buzzwords for key financial measures, e.g., EBIT, OI, OI%, DCF, ROI, PCF, VAT, WIN, and hundreds more. Make sure that you know what they all are—which is easy to do with a quick search on the Internet—and then use that to decode how your local finance guru explains the numbers. Sometimes the locally applied measure does not match the "industry standard," and could put you in an awkward situation. The distinction between "margin" and "markup" still gives me fits when trying to explain it. Practice your story so it conforms to our Scrappy Principle—simple and sensible.

Mind the GAAP, It Can Be Taxing

Despite the magic that can occur in the books, there are the Generally Accepted Accounting Principles (GAAP) that all scrupulous finance folks aspire to follow. I don't think there is any need for you as the Scrappy GM to understand these in depth, but you definitely will need a trusted advisor, either within your organization or subcontracted to you, that does. There are slight variations between companies and countries, but, in general, everyone follows the basic rule set, and more global standards are on the way, thanks to the 2008 "Lehman Shock" and other nasty events.[36] In my experience, the only area that seems to move about is guidelines on what can be capitalized to the balance sheet and depreciated over a number of years, versus what must be expensed in the current financial year. Find a financial expert you trust to guide you through the rules and regulations, then use your GM judgment to make decisions informed by their financial analysis.

"A fine is a tax for doing something wrong. A tax is a fine for doing something right!"
– Author Unknown

When it comes to dealing with taxes, there's no choice but to get professional help. Again, depending on the size of your organization, this may be in-house or external. The tax laws are different from country to country, and the one thing that's constant is ongoing change to those laws. Don't skimp on this—you'll definitely need a specialist's help to keep up! Ethically speaking, the aim of the Scrappy GM is to be paying only what is fair and due to Mr. Taxman, but definitely not a shred more.

---

36. Alistair Milne, *The Fall of the House of Credit: What Went Wrong in Banking and What Can Be Done to Repair the Damage?* (Cambridge University Press, 2009).

Collecting the Cash/Paying the Bills and Your Staff

Life is good when you've got great revenue and margins, but it's an entirely different world when the cash isn't coming in the door quickly enough—or at all. First, you need customers of course. Happy customers will pay their bills, so if you've delivered well, there's usually no problem collecting your fee (unless your customers are sliding into a financial quagmire). If you've delivered well and the bill isn't being paid, you shouldn't feel uncomfortable chasing payment down. Cash is king! The quicker you can get your revenue in the door the better.

The converse is obviously true when it comes to making payments. The longer you can hang onto your cash before paying bills, the better. (Amazon.com has made a strategic advantage out of this, with growing volumes, customers paying in advance of shipment, and payment to vendors stretching out to three months or more!) However it is very un-Scrappy to unreasonably withhold payment. Any delayed payment should be negotiated, and not come as a surprise to the other party. Short-paying your bills (paying less than the full amount demanded) is a method often used to attempt to gain leverage in resolving disputes. You'll need to make a judgement call on this tactic. Generally speaking, I've not seen it bring any positive outcomes towards dispute resolution, and often I think it just further winds people up. The Harvard Negotiation Project has proven long ago that hardball negotiation tactics, of which short-paying is one, are less effective than "principled negotiation," which is a win-win approach to joint problem-solving for mutual benefit.[37]

Delayed, or non-payment, of wages and salaries to your people is not at all Scrappy, and will quickly backfire. Delaying or skipping payment to yourself is just fine, however, assuming you are not violating any minimum wage laws. And if the whole executive team feels an irresistible urge to donate their salary to the company during a tough period, even better. Our executive editor and her executive team did just that at a start-up that lost their funding during the 2001 Silicon Valley meltdown. This enabled the other twenty-five employees to have a month's notice, with pay, that the company was shutting down.

---

37. Carl Lyons, *I Win, You Win: The Essential Guide to Principled Negotiation* (A & C Black, 2007).

These kinds of symbolic acts can boost morale. Employees are encouraged when executives take personal responsibility for the economic hardships of the company they are leading, instead of laying off their workers or slinking off into the night with a hefty golden parachute when times get tough.

Ethics—Some People Still Live By Them!

"Do unto others as you would have them do unto you."
– *Jesus of Nazareth*

Ethical behavior boils down to having the intent to do what is right, and then aligning your actions to your intent. The results don't always work out favorably, but this is a good place to start. Usually the law in any given country will be a rough guide to what is considered ethical behavior in that particular country, but there are times when you are faced with choices that are legal but not ethical.

While many people see ethical issues as sometimes tricky to work through, I think that it's really quite simple. If you follow the Golden Rule of "do unto others, as you would have them do unto you," you can't go far wrong.

But why bother with ethical behavior? Why not try and take the maximum legal advantage of any situation? Well, unethical behavior is really short-term thinking, and sooner or later it catches up with you. Social networking, such as blogging, ensures that the catch-up period is considerably shorter than it's ever been before. My belief is that people in general are basically well intentioned, and, therefore, they will naturally prefer to deal with organizations that have high ethical and moral values, either as a customer, or as an employee. If you want to continue to attract both employees and customers, develop a reputation for being fair and reasonable.

Legal Compliance and Legislation

Getting in place the legal paperwork is all part of starting a business engagement. Just like a marriage, you need to have the wedding vows done before you party and go on the honeymoon. Once again, depending on your organization's size, working the T's and C's (Terms and Conditions) may be done in-house, or with external help. Good legal and contract help will take the approach that this is all preventative maintenance. Ideally, the only time the completed contract will see the light of day is when it's held high for the celebration photos. The objective is that the clauses in the contract will never be looked at, and certainly never enacted. When negotiating the contracts, you need to seek common ground and avoid having head-to-head confrontation. You certainly do not want contract negotiations to be viewed by your legal counsel and contracts people as "sport." Remember, if it's a sport, your business engagement is the ball, and the less it's thrown, hit, or kicked around the field, the better shape it will be in when the game is over.

Just about every contract negotiation that I've been involved in has key discussions around what I call "the legal ham, cheese, and tomato sandwich": IP, insurance, and liability/indemnity. Often, particularly with large U.S. organizations, they like that sandwich toasted, with fries and a Coke on the side, starting with unlimited liability regimes. With little emotion, I sit back and watch the dance to the legal music jangling in my head. Usually you can work through these ridiculous starting positions and get to a reasonable compromise... usually. But there have been times that it's been a deal killer, stone dead. Accept it and move on. That's all you can do. (Or Scrappy it up by trying to use someone else's contract to get the work under way!) But don't sign contracts with ruinous clauses! You might actually have to live up to them. Likewise, don't ask others to sign contracts you don't fancy you'd ever want to enforce.

As for legal compliance, there is no choice when it comes to legislation. Comply and get on with running your business.

Knowledge Management—Corralling Your Valuable IP

Next to your staff, your intellectual property (IP) is your most valuable asset. Except for the equipment and stock inventory, your business is of no tangible value without it. So how do you get that IP recorded somewhere and kept up to date? Discipline! Frequent review and revision is required.

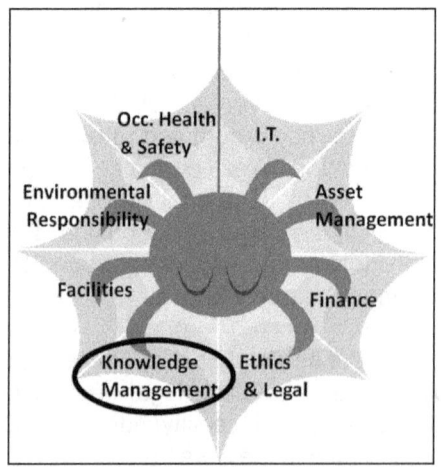

There has to be a little bit of updating done often. I think the common mistake in this area is that 90 percent of the effort is expended on designing and maintaining the repository, while only 10 percent of the effort is spent on the actual data maintenance. Turn those statistics on their head—take the attitude of not caring so much about the repository. Care about the information contained within. As long as you can access the data, update it, and back it up, it doesn't matter whether it's a spreadsheet or a fancy portal-driven document management system. It's the IP that's valuable.

SCRAPPY TIP: Regular meetings to review the information are a great incentive for everyone to get their IP updates in. There's nothing like a bit of peer pressure to sharpen the focus on this key area.

Facilities—Parking Spaces and Toilet Cleaning

I don't know about you, but I'd love to work in a really hip office building—something like a converted, downtown red brick warehouse, with lots of internal glass and steel mezzanines, leather lounges, swanky lighting, and Italian coffee—the ones you see in the TV crime investigation shows. But I don't.

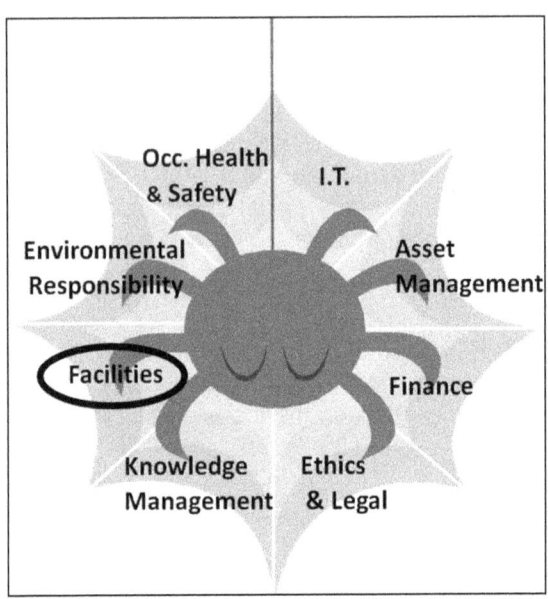

TV is fun. Reality is cruel, so let's get pragmatic. Location is key. You need to get yourself as close to your revenue source as possible, to facilitate easy face-to-face communication with your clients. There's no doubt that this isn't absolutely necessary in this day and age with all the electronic means of communication. However, we're all intrinsically lazy, and it seems to take more effort to set up electronic meetings rather than to just stroll up the street and have an in-person chat (maybe because electronic meetings need to be set up via email, which people have a habit of ignoring). And if your sales people have to battle for an hour or more in traffic to get to a face-to-face meeting, they're far less likely to do it.

There has been a recent trend to moving offices out away from the central business districts and, as a consequence, away from the clients. Maybe I'm just living in the past, but chatting face-to-face seems to me to be many times more effective than the plastic conversations on a video conference, let alone telephone or an email exchange. If it's expensive to locate near your clients, look at methods of taking up less space. If you're serious about driving a market-oriented culture, you need to be physically close to your customers. Whichever way you look at it, face-to-face driven revenue will outstrip any cost savings that can be achieved by being located out in the boondocks, so work it out! And if your customers are a plane ride away, put lots of plane tickets in the budget, and make sure your people use them!

Miracles can be achieved by interior architects with office layouts, providing they keep their impulses for deep artistic expression under control. I've never been a fan of the open plan layouts (rows of desks, divided by chest level partitions, no offices). They tend to be cold, and stifle conversation and creativity. You want an environment where people feel comfortable to interact, but can also get some peace to get on with their work when they need to without resorting to wearing ear plugs and taping off their desk space with "DO NOT CROSS" police ribbon. A sensible compromise can be achieved by a good designer, and pretty much anything with four walls and a roof can be made into a functional environment for your business with a little imagination.

Office grumbles are usually around dirty toilets and messy kitchens. These problems are easily managed, so have a solution to avoid them, such as a middle-of-the-day visit by the cleaners. And high blood pressure can be triggered by someone parking in someone else's "reserved" spot. Plenty of parking is but an early heaven for a GM, and, if it's free, it can be an attractive benefit for recruiting and retaining employees.

Although you're very likely focused on bringing in the next lucrative contract, as a GM you do deal with facilities issues. So when evaluating premises, consider location, plenty of parking, or easy access to public transportation. These are the most important ingredients to an office that supports your business needs, and they can't be fixed by a designer or an architect after you've moved in. Almost everything else can be sorted out with a bit of creativity and good planning, maintenance, and facilities management.

Clean, Lean, Green, and Not So Mean

This is an area that is going to occupy increasing prominence in our minds and businesses. It's also an area that makes a lot of sense, as there is usually a win on the business front as well as for the environment—it's "going green." At present, being proactively "green" is largely voluntary, and mainly about being a good business citizen.

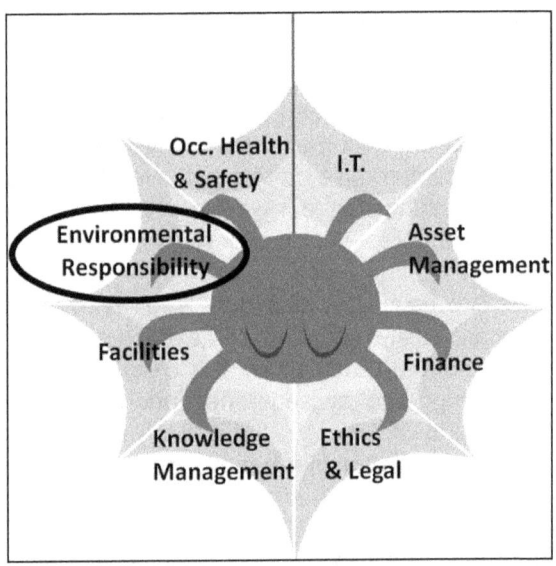

But there's no doubt that, in the very near future, this activity and your business's carbon footprint will be monitored, with the inevitable reductions and thresholds being mandated by governments.

For now, I think there are plenty of straightforward and positive actions that can be taken, for example, monitoring and switching off of anything that consumes power when it is not being used in your business. The monitoring and switching can be done remotely and automatically, with many vendors willing to implement this for very little up front in exchange for a cut of the savings.

I hadn't mentioned "hot desking" (sharing of office accommodations) and virtual workers in the previous section on facilities because I've left them a special little spot here. Why? These are your real (as in not a pipe dream) low hanging fruit in the quest to reduce the carbon footprint in your organization. In most cases, people's personal carbon footprint does not increase much if they are working from home. And if you're not replicating space, power, heating, air-conditioning, and all the other resources it takes to accommodate a person in the workplace, then there has to be immediate savings to your business. Additionally, the person isn't commuting to work, which saves greenhouse gases there.

I've mentioned cloud computing previously in this chapter. It's also a fantastic, easily achievable way to reduce your business' carbon and physical footprint.[38] If you have the security and cultural factors under control, there's no reason why this shouldn't be exploited right now.

Finally, any activity in this area is great PR fodder, being a plus no matter what angle someone wants to view it from. So I don't think there are any excuses—get your greening of the business program underway and reap the benefits, both financial and in your enhanced reputation!

OH&S—Caution, Work May Be Hazardous to Your Health!

Solid practices in occupational health and safety are a plus for everyone—employee, employer and customer. A well-run program will help towards reducing injury and illness, and keep your employees where you want them to be—healthy and happy at work.

---

38. John Lamb, *The Greening of IT: How Companies Can Make a Difference for the Environment* (IBM Press, 2009).

Most countries have legislative requirements that ensure the general physical well being and safety of your people, but there are a couple of other areas to be considered that aren't likely to be included in that legislation.

Preventative Maintenance: In most developed countries now there is a growing issue of an aging workforce and a more sedentary lifestyle (translation: we're getting old and fat). Prevention is better than a cure, so I think it's a great idea to organize workplace—based general health checks for your people, arranging for it to be done at no charge to the employee. It's better to find out that someone is at risk of having a heart attack and have them do something about it, than to wait until you have to call the ambulance. Raising awareness shows you care (one of the top most motivating factors for employees), and inspires self-motivated health improvements.[39] We carry out "healthy heart checks" in our offices each year, and in the weeks following there are usually more gym bags in the office, and less chocolate sold from the vending machines... but only for a couple of weeks. Look for ways to keep people healthy and happy year round. Usually there's at least one health nut in the office who'd gladly take this on as an extracurricular activity with a small budget. It's well worth the investment.

---

39. Bob Nelson, *1001 Ways to Reward Employees* (Workman Publishing Company, 1994).

Silent Suffering: Whatever the reason (perhaps it's as simple as increased awareness) there seems to be a greater prevalence of people suffering from depression-related issues in our modern workplaces. The causes may or may not be workplace related, but the symptoms will most surely affect the person's work performance. The tricky part is that typically these people will not step forward and seek help. A proactive approach is required to ensure that the help they need is readily available, and also to have an awareness program that will encourage people to keep an eye out both for themselves and for each other. That top performer who suddenly misses a deadline or flubs a big client deliverable might need a friendly ear and a shoulder to cry on, not a reprimand.

"Sometimes our light goes out, but is blown again into flame by an encounter with another human being. Each of us owes the deepest thanks to those who have rekindled this inner light."
– Albert Schweitzer

The Oldest Web—The Web of Relationships

We've covered a lot of ground here. It's not necessarily the part of the job with the highest viz or the most glamour, but these areas are fundamental to your business success. And it's clear that, per Ross Perot's quote at the start of the chapter, there's a web of relationships, processes, and structures that are needed to support any business. They might seem like mundane areas not worthy of much attention, but don't be fooled, as whenever I've let these fundamentals slip, they've always come back to bite me. So don't accept the status quo and dodgy old carpet, doing things just as the past three generations of GMs have done. Constantly shift, tune, course-correct, and change. Keep everyone on their toes and energized!

Wrap Up—Now It's Your Turn to Get Scrappy!

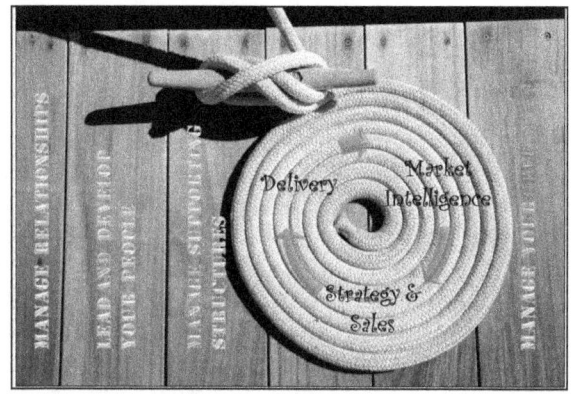

"Act as if you have already achieved your goal-and it's yours!"
– *Dr. Robert Anthony, Self-Help Author*

One of my favorite inspirational stories is that of Burt Munro, the New Zealander made famous by the movie, *The World's Fastest Indian*.[40] Burt was a man of modest means, but dreamt of breaking the world speed record for motorcycles of under 1,000cc engine capacity (Figure 16).

---

40. *The World's Fastest Indian* (Magnolia Pictures, 2005).

Photo from Wikipedia

Figure 16: Burt and His "Munro Special"

Burt tinkered in his shed, making continuous improvements over many decades to a 1920s Indian Scout motorcycle that had an original top speed of only 55 mph. All the changes and improvements eventually enabled Burt to capture several land speed records in the 1960s. In 1969, he achieved an unbelievable speed of 205 mph at Bonneville Speed Week on the salt flats in Utah, riding the same Indian motorcycle that he started tinkering with in 1926. So, what's some old coot and motorcycle speed records have to do with running a business? On the surface, not much. What's important, though, is the attitude and approach that Burt took which enabled him to achieve goals that initially seemed impossible and which surely attracted plenty of well-meaning advice over the decades about what a waste of time it all was.

Burt was indeed a very Scrappy fellow. If we compare the processes that old Burt went through to those that a Scrappy General Manager would use to run a business, we can find many parallels. He understood the lay of the land and clearly understood his competition. The goal theory of motivation was alive and kicking within Burt. He'd set and reset strategies to achieve his goals and took the time to track his progress against them. He demonstrated great leadership skills, being able to elicit enthusiastic and freely-given support from people who eagerly teamed up with him to help him reach his goals. *The World's Fastest Indian* also depicted a character that greatly enjoyed life, and, while at times Burt would work through the night on projects, he was able to achieve a decent amount of balance in his life. This gave him the stamina to keep working steadily towards his goals over many decades (not that a Scrappy GM would be expected to do forty years in the job... being a GM is not a life sentence!). What struck me most about Burt's forty years of devotion and unlikely success was his attitude. This may very well be the most powerful tool in Burt's toolbox, and in the Scrappy GM's toolbox, too. While many circumstances that impact your business are largely out of your control, you and your team always have a choice of what attitude to take. If you want to be a winner like Burt, choose a positive one, and make that attitude positively infectious.

My own approach to running a business has been similar to Burt's approach to getting his motorcycle to go faster. It can always be improved, but I don't try and boil the ocean in one go, nor do I throw my bike in the bush and start again from scratch. There's constant tuning and alteration, with no part being sacred. What can't be improved can be replaced. What's not needed can be done without. Where there's failure, you've learned. Where there's success, there's something to keep and reset the baseline to continue improving from. Above all, I find there's something deeply calming and satisfying in the knowledge that you've been entrusted with running a business that so many people depend on for their livelihoods—and that you've done it well.

In keeping things running well and improving in your business, the processes described in this book will need to be repeated continually, year in and year out. It doesn't matter whether your business is large or small; these processes apply in much the same way. At the start of each chapter in this book there's a picture of rope coiled on the planks of a dock. This symbolizes the continuous cycle of gathering **market intelligence**, setting **strategy**, engaging in **sales and marketing**, and then **delivering** what was sold. The cycle is supported by the "planks" of **managing relationships**, **leading your people**, **managing yourself**, and having the required **supporting structures** in place.

When all of these processes and cycles are followed, growth and success will be possible, despite the prevailing economic conditions. Even in a shrinking market, you can still take market share away from your competitors and grow. And when the good times come along, you'll be water skiing while everyone else is treading water—or, like Burt, speeding like a rocket on a 1920s motorcycle.

Keep it Scrappy!
– Michael

About the Author

Michael Horton is Vice President for the Australian Chemical, Energy, and Natural Resources division of Computer Sciences Corporation (CSC), with responsibility for annual revenues of $360 million and a matrix responsibility for 2,000 people. Michael has 28 years experience in the Information Technology Industry, 21 years of that in a management capacity and has been employed at CSC since 1994. During his time at CSC, he has held senior management positions in Western Australia, Victoria and New South Wales, Australia. Since 2000 he has also completed challenging assignments based in Singapore, Kuala Lumpur, Malaysia, Maidstone in the UK and San Diego, USA.

Michael holds an Associate Diploma in Applied Science from Edith Cowan University in Western Australia, a Master of IT Management from Charles Sturt University in New South Wales and is Project Management Institute (PMI) certified. He is married, with two teenage children and enjoys surfing, sailing and holidaying at every opportunity.

Books

Other Happy About® Books

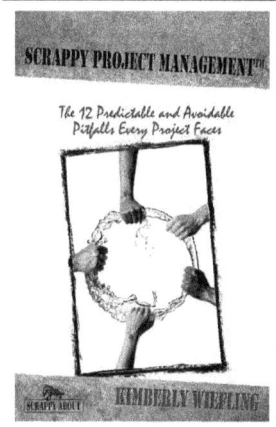

Scrappy Project Management

This book is for people who need to get things done...especially project managers.

Paperback $19.95
eBook $14.95

Climbing the Ladder of Business Intelligence

The purpose of this book is to introduce and guide the reader through a framework that enables a business to organize itself intelligently.

Paperback:$19.95
eBook: $14.95

Purchase these books at Happy About
http://happyabout.info
or at other online and physical bookstores.

Scrappy Women in Business

Each chapter is a fascinating description of one woman's unlikely journey, and every story is teeming with personal insights and practical tips to encourage you along the way toward your own goals and dreams.

Paperback $19.95
eBook $14.95

42 Rules™ of Employee Engagement

This book takes a practical, straightforward and fun look at what it takes to build community, commitment and a culture of engagement in the business world today.

Paperback $19.95
eBook $14.95

CPSIA information can be obtained
at www.ICGtesting.com
Printed in the USA
FSHW011014101019
62758FS